Five Gifts of Pro-Aging

Five Gifts of Pro-Aging

*Honoring Maturity in a
Culture That Could Use It*

M ARCIA N EWMAN

BALBOA.
PRESS

A DIVISION OF HAY HOUSE

Balboa Press books may be ordered through booksellers or by contacting:

Balboa Press
A Division of Hay House
1663 Liberty Drive
Bloomington, IN 47403
www.balboapress.com
1 (877) 407-4847

Printed in the United States of America.

ISBN: 978-1-4525-9543-6 (sc)
ISBN: 978-1-4525-9542-9 (e)

Library of Congress Control Number: 2014906130

Balboa Press rev. date: 06/30/2014

Dedication

To the Breath of Life from which all blessings flow
To Jim who helps keep it fun and real
And to my caring & collaborative Sister-Friends

Contents

Introduction

I live in the epicenter of a youthquake—the village of Los Angeles. It is an adventurous, quirky land filled with youth worshiping folk. We've turned into a species who are desperately trying to find their happy in a wrinkle-free existence. Any normal visible sign of aging is seen as a huge curse that must be lifted, literally. I counsel many women who are struggling with the reality of their aging. Increasingly, they have become obsessively caught in the insatiable practice of nip, tuck, highlight, laser and fill. To use a highly sophisticated therapist term—*it's plain nuts.*

I too got caught up. When my own aging reality hit me like a Mack truck, it knocked the wind out of my youthfulness. In fact, this book was born out of my own aging crisis. Quite honestly, I didn't think I would ever struggle with the concept of becoming older. Somehow I thought I'd be immune to these conflicts since I was a well seasoned psychotherapist and wellness coach. Over a span of twenty-five plus years I had counseled a multitude of clients going through life's transitions, many of them high-functioning women. I took pride in my healthy support system and my ninja-level practices of personal growth. Regardless of it all, my own aging drama arrived—right on schedule. The *Reality Reaper* pounded heavily on my front door with its list of demands.

It's been my experience the more you avoid facing the inevitable, the harder it becomes. Eventually, I did surrender and finally opened that thick, terrifying door. Surprisingly, I was able to look beyond the *Reality Reaper's* haggard face, saggy eyelids and glimpse into the real light of my own eyes. What I found was this; *life had not abandoned me.*

When I opened that thick door, death also paid me a visit. I had to fully face and accept my own mortality and those of my loved ones. In fact, my own father transitioned out of his physical body while writing this book. Months earlier, soon after his cancer diagnosis, I was speaking with my dad on the phone. He announced casually "Oh, I want you to know in three months I'll be gone" and then proceeded to talk about the Green Bay Packers.

Thank goodness, I listened to him (this time). I took a leave from my private practice and we spent some very precious time together. Right through his last breath, a palpable presence of grace surrounded my father and our family. And yes, it was three months later when he transitioned out of his body. Each day of my life has become increasingly precious to me now. I have found a gentler and saner way to live with the reality of what is.

Is joy-filled aging really possible? *Five Gifts of Pro-aging* is to help spark that possibility in each one of us. You'll find a re-occurring theme in the pages ahead; ***if you live consciously, you will age more comfortably.*** The purpose of this book is to help you swim strongly in this life, especially through these rip-tides of our current aging-phobic world. Even though this guidebook was written primarily for midlife American women, it contains universal themes that can benefit any human being around the globe. My role is to help foster and navigate pro-aging consciousness for those who are interested in a fulfilling life. Being "over the hill" takes on new meaning when the view is divine.

As American Boomer women, we are the perfect ones to revolutionize the aging freedom movement. It is my joy and privilege to bring this labor of love into the mix. My vision holds a brighter, more mature culture where women are able to receive full human dignity, no matter one's chronological age. Thank you for your interest and for passing along this timely pro-aging message. Most of all, my hope is that you recognize how truly awesome you already are.

CHAPTER ONE

The Gift of Authenticity

"After a certain number of years, our faces become our biographies."
—CYNTHIA OZICK

W e are part of seventy-eight million Baby Boomers who have changed the course of equal rights and social empowerment for women and minorities around the world. Yet, take notice of how very narrow the range of acceptable looks for women have become. In Southern California where I live, the range is even narrower, stemming from a culture of intense age phobia. It appears that the unnatural has become the new natural.

Most American women wish the media would do a better job of portraying us with more diverse physical attractiveness, including age, shape and size. In fact, according to AdMedia.com, only five percent of women in the United States actually fit the current body type popularly portrayed in advertising today. I use to be one of those who fantasized about the 'media good-fairy' arriving one day soon. Then I decided to take matters into my own hands, starting with my own scalp.

Never in my life did I think I'd write a book that begins with the subject of hair. After all, it seems like such a mundane, superficial topic. Doesn't it? Not really. Hair matters and American women know it. Our hair color and style serves as a walking calling card. It eliminates the need of an elevator speech by directly communicating *this is who I want you to think I am.* As Nora Ephron once proclaimed, "After all, the big difference between our mothers and us is only chemical."

In 1950, fewer than ten percent of American women colored their hair. Today, in the United States there are forty million American women now in their 40's and 50's. A vast majority of these women will spend their money, time and energy on the ritual of hair-dyeing. The estimated range of all the American women who color their hair is eighty to forty percent of the population, depending on which part of the country you live in.

Free Your Hair, the Rest Will Follow

My own story took a hair-pin turn when I decided to stop coloring it at the age of forty-two. It was the year of 2000. Funny, how it sounded like such a good idea at the time. I was really motivated for two primary reasons. First, I wanted to stop putting more chemical toxins into my body. Secondly, I wanted to save some bucks and put that increasingly pricey salon money into other things. Looking back, I was so pleased with my smart la-di-da plan of allowing my hair to go *au-natural.*

Everything seemed to be in a perfect place for my simple plan to proceed. I took great reassurance that my professional background would carry me through this "hair transition" quite easily. At the time, I was filled with extra bravado since I had relocated to Florida to be with my new love. I took comfort in the fact in my years of daily meditation. "I thought, what's the big deal? I just won't dye my hair anymore. I can handle this. I'll just quickly address any aging stuff that may come up. Right?"

Wrong. I was so very, very wrong. I was not prepared for the intense negativity that came my way. As I looked in the mirror, I'd hear this shrieking voice inside say: "PLEASE-MAKE-THIS-AGING-MONSTER-GO-AWAY!" For months and months, I questioned my daily sanity when a simple visit to my hair colorist would make it all go away (or so I thought).

The *Aging-Reality Reaper* was certainly having her way with me. The dark thoughts of extreme self doubt and paranoia were my frequent visitors. I had finally come face-to-face with my own ageism. My egoic mind was filled with such revulsion about growing visibly older. It kept feeding me insidious questions. *Why I was letting myself go? What were other people thinking of me? How come I have to be so different? What am I trying to prove? Can I really do this?*

My bathroom mirror became living proof that I was turning into my mother. As each silver hair multiplied, I had to face each trashy belief and judgment that I held inside. Truthfully, it felt as if my psyche had tapped into a collective unconscious database of our entire age-discriminating society. In the depths of that difficult download, I eventually began to retrieve new information. Remarkably, a wise inner voice prevailed. It brought me this loving, gentle and consistent message: *Just let yourself be, let your hair and your life follow its course.* And so I did. I freed my hair and the rest of the story follows.

age·ist, adjective, noun

age·ism, noun

1. Discrimination against persons of a certain age group.

2. A tendency to regard older persons as debilitated, unworthy of attention, or unsuitable for employment.

Origin:

1965–70; age + -ism, on the model of sexism, racism, etc.
Dictionary.com Unabridged
Based on the Random House Dictionary, © Random House, Inc. 2013.

Swimming Against the Tide

When I decided to free my hair (and face my ageist self) there were no guidebooks in sight. Anne Kreamer's informative book—*Going Gray,* surfaced only a few years ago. Her brave and humorous sentiments mirrored many of my own thoughts. She writes "Did I really think that overnight I'd turn into Barbara Bush or Queen Elizabeth? Because of my fears, I decided that giving up artificial hair color was exactly the right thing for me to do. I've always hated being told by anyone the choices I must make and the ways I must act…by a media-induced cultural hysteria that gray equals desiccated, unsexy and over (the hill). Letting my hair go natural…I was about to find what it felt like to swim against the tide."

Melissa Etheridge, after finishing her cancer treatments, made a brave and bald headed Grammy appearance in 2005. In a later interview she said, "I have a beautiful head of hair…I do dye it blonde, though. I can be bald in front of the world, but I can't be gray."

After I heard about this interview, I thought if a strong, talented, outspoken, feminist and openly gay woman can't bring herself to show her gray to the world, what the #*$@! does that mean for the rest of us westernized women? It shows us what we're up against. And this powerful anti-aging perspective is continuing to build, especially for women in America.

There is another path and it's called healthy pro-aging. To begin, it requires the application of these three tools: Awareness. Awareness. Awareness.

Toxins for Sale

Women who dye their hair have been tested in labs*. What did they find?

Diaminobenzene stuck to their DNA. Diaminobenzene is an extremely toxic substance that is found in conventional hair dyes and many shampoos. This toxin is linked to neurological disorders and disruptions to our endocrine (hormonal) systems.

While we're on the topic of toxins; check all of your hair and skin care product labels and avoid the following ingredients: Sodium Lauryl Sulfate (SLS), Sodium Laureth Sulfate (SLES), Petroleum, Paraffin, Mineral Oil, Paraben, Propylen Glycol, Phthalates, Toluene and Dioxane.

If you can't pronounce what's on the label, don't buy it. Keep it simple and pure.

Remember, what you put on your scalp and skin goes directly into your bloodstream.

If it's not safe to eat your hair dye, toothpaste or shampoo, don't buy it and don't use it.

Campaign for Safe Cosmetics & the Environmental Working Group

---

Ph.D. in Image Management

Starting in my early thirties, I began using artificial (toxic) hair coloring. The maintenance of my darkened hair became a vehicle of personal control and equilibrium. When my sister died, and years later going through a divorce, I needed a sense of stability in my life. I attempted to use my youthful (darker) hair and body fitness to reflect to others and the outside world that "I'm fine. Everything is OK". My Ph.D. could have been in image management. I was cleverly cheating the passage of time (or so I thought). I continued to color my hair because I wasn't ready to look my age, yet. Also, at the time I didn't see any healthy alternatives. Looking around, I witnessed the floundering of many of my gray-haired elders. They appeared to be caught like a trapped fly in a thick web of the victim-decline model of aging. So I chose to stay married to what I knew best—my youth.

It's been my ongoing experience that the ego is a trickster and a manipulator. It often tries to fool others into thinking we are a certain way; younger, richer, more clever, and emotionally stronger than we truly are. That is why the *Reality Reaper* must visit repeatedly, if necessary, to help us become more real. I found there is no way to cheat her. The *Reality Reaper's* job is to mark time, challenge the ego and remind us that no one gets out of here alive. The good news is that her initial visit led me to the first of five precious gifts—an appreciation for more personal authenticity.

When I finally made the decision to no longer mask my white hairs, my salt and pepper hair became a new visual cue to the world. I was no longer young. Growing up as the "baby" of four children, it was a shock to realize that I was actually getting old. Even certain family members reacted negatively to my un-dyed hair since they were more comfortable seeing me a certain way (younger). Fortunately, I come from a Midwest farm family where most of the multi-generational women (and men) didn't see a need to color their hair. According to farmer logic, if you're lucky enough to be aging it means you're still alive and above ground. And that's a good thing. Even today, my eighty-plus white-haired mother (and a great grandmother) can still run golf cart circles around me. She is a prime, energetic example of a healthy pro-ager.

What is Pro-Aging?

Pro-Aging is a fresh response to an anti-aging culture that targets women to find their value in remaining youthful looking. The message of pro-aging is dedicated to helping American Baby Boomer's pioneer healthier aging attitudes and actions. The vision of pro-aging holds a brighter, more mature culture where women are able to receive full human dignity, no matter one's chronological age.

Pro-ager's find they spend less of their precious resources on maintaining youthful appearances and more time enjoying the fruits of their maturity. Healthy pro-ager's naturally seek joyful collaboration on endeavors that restore our humanity, our planet and make a meaningful difference in the hearts of all.

Center Stage

When working with corporate and entertainment industry women, one of the most common themes I hear is the undeniable pressure to look the part, in order to stay in the game. This usually equates to stomping out any signs of aging as quickly as they appear. After working many years in the entertainment industry, author Anne Kreamer provides this truth-filled commentary "Just as Mick Jagger and Paul McCartney believe they have to remain frozen in a circa 1970's groovy-guy look, so too do the executives, who operate businesses that sell music, TV and movies to people of their grandchildren's generation…when it comes to hair color and holding on to dear life to a slight illusion of youthfulness, they are nearly as fear-driven and tyrannized as woman."

A few years ago, I decided to get back into a passion of mine—theatre acting. In rehearsals, I'm often the only person on stage who isn't coloring their hair and that includes the men. One of my Hollywood coaches supported my continued decision to *not dye* my hair. In fact, he said emphatically "It's a very strong choice!" Of course, I wanted to kiss him. It is also true that with every strong choice, strong ego can follow. Is this about going around expecting more brownie points for wearing my salt and pepper hair? Maybe-probably-yes. It's true that vanity can swing in all directions.

Some of my most challenging age-related moments have occurred on stage. When attending NoHo (North Hollywood) acting classes, my youth obsessed ego began to unravel, one neuro-pathway at a time. I'd share the stage with young professional working actors while looking into their crease-less eyes. Usually, I'd play their mother or grandmother while hearing a host of negative aging commentary—both theirs and mine. It turned out to be a deep life review for me. As I took center stage, my childhood dream of wanting to be a professional actress and dancer was finally acknowledged. Yet, this was not the professional road I had taken. As a well-trained Midwesterner, my strong work-ethic chose the practical path of becoming a school teacher and shortly after becoming a psychotherapist. As I showed up for more adult acting classes, I had to face my deep remorse for not listening to my childhood dream. For many weeks, I allowed myself to feel and release this sadness and regret both on stage and off. Fortunately, these supportive acting classes became my quasi-therapy group. I was able to grieve my youthful vision until I could grieve no more.

In America, we lack safe places to fully grieve and honor our life transitions. We don't have a positive ceremony or ritual to mark the second half of our lives. Instead, we give each other black balloons, throw over-the-hill parties and tell bad jokes in order to cover up how vulnerable, marginalized and discarded we may actually feel.

But My Husband Would Have a Fit!

—A Monologue

I've found that having gray hair can be a form of going bare-naked in public. Even though it's been over fifteen years since I stopped dying my hair, I am still surprised by some of the reactions I get. Typically, it goes something like this. I'm in a public restroom washing my hands and another woman approaches the sink area. She looks and talks to me through the mirror and whispers (always the low whisper), *"I think your hair is marvelous, I wish that I could do that too."* After a slight pause, she adds, *"But my husband would have a fit!"*

Now at this point, the proper thing to do would be to nod, smile and politely say "thank you" and just leave it at that. Right? But no, my alter ego who thinks she's Susan B. Anthony has a desperate need to respond to this whispering woman. After all, she started it. Here's my fantasy exchange. I look through the mirror into the whispering woman's eyes and say:

"Really? Are you trying to convince me that you dye your hair an artificial color and pretend that you're still thirty-five, because of your husbands' feelings? I don't think so. Take it from one who personally and professionally knows how to arm wrestle with the She Devil-of-Denial. Sweetie, your fear has nothing to do with anyone else. So let's just face it, okay? You're aging, I'm aging, and we're all aging. And one day each one of us in this frickin' bathroom will be making our final, final flush."

At this crucial point, I reach for her arm pulling her closely into the mirror towards me. I notice her tense reflected look that says "Oh God, I wish I had never said anything to this crazy lady." My chuckle is soft and throaty because this mama cobra is coiled and poised to make another strike. And then I begin to hear these strange and unfamiliar words come out of me.

"It was we, the people, not we, the white male citizens; nor yet we, the male citizens; but we, the whole people, who formed the Union…women as well as men."

That's when I realize, I'm actually channeling my alter ego, Susan B. Anthony from 1873.

"OK, forget that part for now" I quickly say red-faced to the bathroom lady.

I start again. *"Honey, we women are all drowning in this fishbowl of aging confliction…. Come here and look verrrry closely. YESSSSSSSS, I'm one of those freaks of nature here in the Kingdom of Fake. This is what fifty-five looks like—minus the highlights, nip, tuck, laser and fill. It's a miracle that my nasolabial folds and my errant white hairs are finding their way too. I simply got tired of worshiping a temporary Diva—the Goddess of Youth. Besides, her powers are much over-rated."*

Turning back to the bathroom mirror woman, I exclaim *"WHO-THE-HELL-CARES-IF-YOUR-HUSBAND-HAS-A-FIT!?"* My gentle tirade continues.

"It's your own body. Do you really want to keep poisoning yourself with chemical hair dye? Does it stop there or will you soon jump on the bandwagon of body mutilation practices too? Are you really going to trade-in this PRECIOUS LIFE for some narrow, generic version of femininity and then to top it off—blame it on men!? "

At this point, the bathroom-mirror lady has slowly inched her way to the door. She exits.

I notice her escape and release a slow sigh.

I confess that a part of me is indeed jealous that the bathroom mirror lady can slip so easily into the world of perky breasts and puffy collagen lips. I admit I've never been good at female conformity. I finish drying my hands while glancing down at them and mutter *"Oh damn, I've grown another big brown aging spot."*

The Gray-Roots Movement

More recently, there is a growing trend of women who are celebrating their natural shades of gray, silver or white. Cindy Joseph, a working model with her beautiful signature long, gray hair was signed on to the Ford Models-Classic division, *after* she stopped dyeing her hair. In an interview (*www.boombycindyjoseph.com*), Joseph's contagious pro-aging attitude sums it up beautifully: "Aging is really just another word for living. I'm always and forever in the prime of my life."

Additional supportive resources are popping up like Terri Holley's popular blog, *GoingGrayBlog.com* and Diana Lewis Jewell's *GoingGrayLookingGreat.com*. There's even a Facebook page of *Silver Sisters*—women who tow their own airstream campers. If you see them on the road, don't forget to give them a supportive silver sisters' wink.

On a celebrity level, there are silver-hair pioneers like Jamie Lee Curtis, Emmy Lou Harris, Helen Mirren and Betty White. In addition, I hold huge respect for healthy pro-ager's Meryl Streep, Emma Thompson and Diane Keaton. They exude feminine power while keeping their sense of humor, humility and sensuality alive.

In Betty Friedan's extensive study of aging in *The Fountain of Age* (1993), she beautifully describes how the key to a continued vital involvement in life is to "first adopt an active realistic acceptance of age related changes as opposed to denial or passive resignation. It takes a conscious breaking out of the youthful definitions, for a man or women, to free oneself for continued development."

Carolyn Myss offers an additional pro-aging jewel. "We can no longer allow ourselves to age at the speed of our physical bodies or cease being a creative asset to the whole of life because we have grey hair. Energy—or grace—is an ageless, timeless, and endless resource, no matter the age of the physical body. The myth that we are no longer as valuable as we get older is one I shall be delighted to abandon."

Allowing one's hair to grow gray is just one visible way to express our freedom in an anti-aging culture. If you're interested in discovering more about the gift of authenticity, keep reading. You'll find what fits for you. Let's dive in!

The Aging Awareness Questionnaire

This two-part questionnaire is designed to heighten your aging consciousness. It is also a forum to openly share your experiences about becoming older. As a culture we've been trained to keep this aging stuff under wraps and try to figure it out on our own. Don't be surprised if you find yourself wanting to skim or skip over this section. I highly recommend that you don't. Please be willing to at least read each of the questions. If you're not ready to write out your answers, there's no judgment. You'll be ready when you're ready.

If you're good to go, then grab your journal. I recommend that you set aside 15-30 minutes each day until you've completed all the questions. As you read each question, let it percolate into your being. With as much honesty as you can, write out your responses.

After you have finished answering all of the questions, it is important that you share your responses with a trusted individual. As you open yourself to this inner work, it's preferable that the first person who will be hearing your responses is NOT your spouse, partner or family hamster.

Some of you may prefer to complete this questionnaire in a more guided experience. If that's your preference, join one of my classes, workshops, weekend retreats or request a private consultation. Remember, these study questions can be completed in the privacy of your own home without having to have a group experience. Most importantly, reply to these questions as openly as you can and make sure you find a pro-aging buddy who can hear and honor your responses.

Aging Awareness Questionnaire: Part One

1. What does your hair color say about you?

2. How do you feel about your current age?

3. When did you realize that you were getting older? What happened?

4. Do you feel pressured to look younger from the media, yourself or others?

5. Do you color your hair? Have you ever thought about allowing your hair to return to its natural color?

6. Did you ever try to stop coloring your hair?

7. What thoughts or feelings come up when you see your gray hairs coming through?

8. What would you worry about the most if you stopped dyeing your hair?

9. What do you think of women who let their hair go gray?

10. What do you think of men who dye their hair?

11. What do you think of men who let their hair go gray or become bald?

12. Please write about your feelings regarding these statements;

   "If a man is going gray, it makes them look more distinguished.
   When a woman is going gray, she's letting herself go."

13. Does or did your mother, aunt(s) and grandmother(s) dye their hair? Why or why not, do you suppose?

14. Do you think there is more pressure to look younger than there was fifty years ago?

15. Estimate the number of hours and the total amount of money you've spent on hair coloring appointments and hair-related services in the past year.

16.   Make an estimate of how much money you've spent on the above services through your adult years.

17.   What does being authentic mean to you?

18.   Does it include retaining the natural color of your hair or not?

Congratulations, you made it through Part One. Take a break.

You may want to take a stroll outside into the fresh air. Go throw some rocks, if necessary.

Welcome Back.

Before proceeding with Part Two of the *Aging Awareness Questionnaire,* I've included some background information to help set the tone.

Liposuction 101

The anti-aging market is a very lucrative global industry. By the year 2015, revenue in the global anti-aging market will exceed $200 Billion according to the American Academy of Anti-Aging Medicine. In 2010, while consulting at a prominent addictions center in Malibu, I was indoctrinated into the world of liposuction-thinking. I was privy to conversations of young women with access to lots of cash. Women (under the age of thirty, mind you) disclosed they were turning to surgical liposuction as if it were the latest and greatest diet ever invented. I was stunned. Even with three decades of eating disorder recovery under my own personal belt, this was the first time I had come across this one.

During a group, one young woman turned to me and asked "I'm considering getting more liposuction, what do you think?" The next thing I knew, all eyes were upon me. My uncensored sarcasm showed up first. Fortunately, I throttled it back. But this is how I really wanted to respond to her. *"So what about the fat between your ears? Each brain is 60% fat, it needs fat to function. Shall we suck that out too? Or has all your repeated alcohol and pharmaceutical abuse already wiped out most of your brain cells which govern common sense?"*

Wow. I'm really glad I didn't say that out loud. Instead, I offered this troubled young woman a question. "What is it that you're hoping to feel AFTER you have the liposuction?" She pondered and then replied "I want to look and feel better about my body". I nodded and replied, "Exactly" (while gently leaning forward towards her like a good therapist). "So yes, let's start there. Let's find more ways for you to access better feelings about yourself and your body before you take on any more surgery. That way, if you decide to have more liposuction in the future, you're already in a more positive place going into it. Okay?" She nodded in agreement. I was so pleased to be able to keep my job that day.

Fast forward two years later. I'm facilitating an eating disorders group for adolescent girls at a different treatment facility. I hear these truth-filled words from the mouth of a 14-year old: "My mom and I have a similar body shape. She tells me there's nothing wrong with how I look. But over the weekend she just had some more liposuction. And she'll be back in the gym by Monday for more compulsive exercising. What kind of message does that send me?"

There is a saying from the Talmud that says *"When you teach your daughter, you teach your daughter's daughter.* Obviously, the solution here is deeper than just sucking out one's fat. More American women need to demonstrate that our self esteem can be separate from our body esteem. Cleary, our appearance helps shape our self-image and affects the way that others deal with us. I'm certainly not against looking and feeling good. I still buy a pricey moisturizer and like to eat healthy food. But at what point do our countless attempts at a firm belly and glowing skin distract us from evolving and enjoying the last third of our life? With the gifts of pro-aging, we get to examine our dysfunctional love affair with our "look-a-holic" society.

The 3 B's: Body Checking, BDD & Be Informed

From an early age, we watched our mothers, aunts and sisters stand in front of (or avoid) mirrors. We learned that any reflective surface or tinted window becomes an opportunity to conduct a quick body examination. In passing through each developmental check point, women have been taught to refine our body checking skills. Healthy pro-aging is when a woman finally asks herself, "What do I really need to be checking and measuring?"

American women are obsessed with measuring, especially when it comes to the digital scale. Each time you step on a weight measuring scale you are conducting a body-check. It's possible that body-checking could be a neutral exercise. In my profession, I see that it's rarely the case.

I'm compelled to share this pro-aging message because of the constant self-dissatisfaction I hear coming from women and girls of all ages. I've treated countless women who measure their self-worth based on a digital scale number and their latest BMI (body mass index). Heroically, one local eating disorder treatment center conducts "scale smashing ceremonies" driving home the point of America's preoccupation with body weight measurements. Body checking can also progress into a serious mental condition.

Body Dysmorphic Disorder (BDD) is a type of chronic mental condition (illness) in which one can't stop thinking about a flaw in their appearance—a flaw that is either minor or imagined. Body dysmorphic disorder has sometimes been called "imagined ugliness." Women suffering with BDD feel their appearance is so shameful that they don't want to be seen by others. BDD individuals will intensely obsess over their appearance and body image, often for many hours a day. This preoccupation with appearance causes significant distress or problems in one's social life, work, school and other areas of functioning. In time, many seek out cosmetic procedures to try to 'fix' their perceived flaws but never seem to be satisfied.

Cosmetic procedures do not treat the underlying condition of BDD. Given our cultural stigma against aging and the corresponding rise in plastic surgery, it has become very difficult to provide education, diagnosis and proper treatment of Body Dysmorphic Disorder. At a recent women's conference, I had the opportunity to speak with actress-Jamie Lee Curtis on this growing issue. She relayed her concerns about many of her female celebrity friends who are now caught up in compulsive acts of ongoing plastic surgery. Similar to addictive eating (or not eating), compulsive shopping, gambling, debting or a sex addiction, —ongoing cosmetic surgery and other "rejuvenating" procedures can turn into a compulsive activity or what is called a *process addiction.*

As more women's magazines carry glossy-looking cosmetic surgery advertisements, I'm struck by how these "before" and "after" pictures don't include the nitty gritty. The ads fail to mention how one's face will be sliced open and the facial skin will be stretched (sometimes beyond recognition). Nor do these ads mention the possible lingering pain connected to these "in and out" procedures and the rising number of women who have become hooked on the pain medication they received following cosmetic surgery.

I'm not interested in criticizing those who choose plastic surgery to deal with their aging challenges. I'm an advocate for increasing women's aging awareness. For example, the popular injectibles that are flying off the medical spa shelves, some of these live toxins are now being linked to cancer metastases and the growth of new blood vessels that feed tumors (angiogenesis). In a society that reminds us at every turn that our looks are tremendously important, it's important to do your research before you inject, nip, tuck or suction.

Aging Awareness Questionnaire: Part Two

Thank you for keeping your pen and journal handy. The following questions are designed to help you understand more youthful definitions and any lingering ageist stereotypes. Read each question carefully. Remember to breathe and then write out your honest answers. This is a gentle reminder to not judge your current thoughts and behaviors. Simply witness and accept where you are at, right now.

1. What part(s) of your body do you tend to think needs fixing? How often do you think about this—monthly, weekly, daily, hourly?

2. What do you think of wrinkles?

3. What are you doing to try to delay your aging process?

4. What do you think about our current anti-aging culture? Please comment on the anti-aging influences from the following; mainstream media, cosmetic-beauty industry, pharmaceutical companies, medical spa's, and the entertainment business

5. Have you ever received cosmetic injections or cosmetic surgery?

6. If so, what thoughts led you to that decision?

7. Did your mother, aunt(s) or grandmother receive cosmetic injections or cosmetic surgery?

8. Why do you think they did or didn't?

9. What are you most concerned about if you choose *not* to have cosmetic injections and/or cosmetic surgery?

10. What are you most concerned about if you *do* choose to go ahead with them?

11. What kind of benefits do you get for looking younger?

12. Do you think that these benefits are different for women than they are for men? If so, how? What do you think about that?

13. How much time and money do you spend monthly on anti-aging products, services & treatments?

14. How many of your work hours does it take for you to pay for these services?

15. How do you feel when you noticeably see your friends and family members becoming older?

16. How do you feel when you look in the mirror or see pictures of yourself looking older?

17. List your top five negative thoughts about aging. What do you worry about most?

18. What discriminating ideas have you learned about growing older? Make a list of aging-related stereotypes that you have heard.

19. Which of these aging stereotypes do you believe are true?

20. What are your top 3 regrets? Who do you need to make peace with?

21. Do you ever think your anti-aging efforts could be channeled into other endeavors? If so, what is calling you?

22. Who inspires you when it comes to their life and the aging process? What other resources have you found helpful?

23. Do you think there is a certain age at which you won't care if you look old? If so, what age would you anticipate that would be?

24. On a scale of 1 to 10 where do you think you are in terms of your age acceptance?

    (0 is zero acceptance, 10 is total acceptance).

    Write out a couple of sentences about your answer.

25. On a scale of 1 to 10 where do you think you in terms of your body acceptance?

    (0 is zero acceptance, 10 is total acceptance).

    Write out a couple of sentences about your answer.

26. On a scale of 1 to 10 where are you about accepting the fact of your own mortality?

    (0 is complete denial, 10 is total acceptance)

    Write out a couple of sentences about your answer.

    The *Pro-Aging Visions* exercise provided in Chapter Five will help expand your answers to these final two questions.

27. What new pro-aging beliefs and actions would you like to endorse?

28. If the message of pro-aging could be embraced more in our American society, what changes would we see? How can you help with this change?

Congrats, for finishing your *Aging Awareness Questionnaire*. Remember to share your responses with a pro-aging buddy.

CHAPTER TWO

The Gift of Self-Healing

"It's always darkest before it goes pitch black."
—Anonymous

If you hang around me enough, you'll hear me repeat two important things. Firstly, find a way every day to access and enjoy your true essence. If that sounds incredibly vague to you, keep reading. Secondly, find and practice a simple and effective method of emotional processing. It doesn't really matter if six enlightened Zen Buddhists came up with the technique or not. What's important is that you use one, especially when you least want to.

Processing is an effective tool to help lighten up your daily life. Processing clears emotional reactivity and as a bonus, may help heal a troubling physical condition that may be connected. As Louise Hay's famous saying goes *what you can feel you can heal.* Self-healing is an ongoing practice of acknowledging, welcoming and understanding one's emotions and the thoughts/actions behind them.

With the accelerated pace of our current world, an untrained mind can be a dangerous thing. Let's face it. We each have an inner critic who's like a mean little seventh grader. Don't tell me you haven't noticed her. She's the nasty, bully-type who judges and doubts most everything. In the process of living longer we now have the opportunity to finally reconcile with our inner cast of characters, including our critical seventh grader or her polar opposite—the anxious victim.

Self-healing involves taking personal stock every single day. In these crazy times of increased world chaos, it is so easy to point out the negativity and insanity of others. Don't fall for that continued distraction. Bring yourself back to home base. The word *Heal* means to 'set right or repair'. It is about healing our personal self, not our troubled neighbor, conflicted cousin, or a lousy boss. **Conscious pro-aging is being able to look at our part and see what we are contributing to the moment.**

The gift of self-healing is about allowing a gentler, kinder power to find what it wants to heal—beyond our ego's agenda. When emotional processing is compassionately practiced, it will help you to focus on your inner pureness. We then evolve into the human beings that we came here to be. Our true nature consists of these higher states of being: humility, forgiveness, gratitude, kindness, generosity, unconditional love, joy and contentment.

If you haven't found a simple and effective emotional processing technique, you can borrow mine. In brief, it is a body-mind based approach that I use with clients. It's portable and simple enough for anyone to learn within a few minutes.

Body-Mind Processing Method (BMPM)

» Close your eyes and breathe. Focus on your breath coming in and out.

» Drop your awareness down into your body, breathing all the way down into your lower stomach and hips.

» Welcome whatever feeling arises. Silently to yourself or out loud, let the feeling know that it is welcomed and acceptable to be here right now. Practice non-judgment of the emotion. Welcome the feeling.

» Notice your body sensations. Notice where in your body you are holding this feeling. You may be holding the feeling in several locations in your body and/or you may be experiencing several emotions at once.

» FACE the feeling, FEEL the feeling. Go right into the belly of the emotion, if possible.

» If you find yourself frozen (numb), not wanting to feel or you're fighting this process, keep repeating the steps above. Allow yourself to gently settle into your body with the rhythm of the breath.

» If helpful, place your hand or both hands on the area(s) to help with your focus (this step is optional).

» Notice if there is an image, color, word, or sentence that emerges from your awareness.

» Whatever comes up, practice non-judgment as best as you can. See yourself with this emotion and sensations from the eyes of unconditional love.

» Stay with it until you discover the core message of this visiting feeling. Understand what current thought (belief) may be attached to this feeling.

» Thank it for visiting. Then watch and notice if and how the feeling/thoughts transforms into something else or simply dissolves away.

» If you are experiencing a highly reactive situation, you may gain more benefit by writing down your responses, as you move through each of the above steps.

For Advanced Processing

» Decide if you're comfortable holding on to this current belief and feeling. If not, select an improved thought and feeling, one that provides you more relief.

» Introduce this new thought and feeling into your body-mind. You may choose to write it down on paper and read it out loud.

» Breathe and notice the contrast of how this new and improved thought feels in your body.

Client Example: Using Body-Mind Processing Method (BMPM)

Jill, a 54 year old business analyst comes into my office with growing dissatisfaction of her corporate work. Her symptoms include exhaustion and muscular tension. I introduce her to the Body-Mind Processing Method.

» Jill sits quietly in her chair, connecting with each breath—in and out.

» She's been avoiding her anger that she feels toward a narcissistic co-worker who continues to emotionally manipulate their shared boss. I ask her to just feel the anger.

» She becomes hyper-verbal in her talking, intellectualizing the situation. Jill is stuck in her head.

» I gently re-direct her to just sit in stillness and allow herself to feel.

» I encourage Jill to welcome the anger and let it know that it is acceptable to be here. After several minutes of silence, Jill is able to affirm to herself, "This anger is welcomed here."

» She begins to identify the center of her anger. She points to her stomach (solar plexus) area where the feeling is the strongest. The solar plexus area often represents our sense of personal power or powerlessness.

» Jill places both hands on her stomach while still feeling more anger as she connects with her breathing.

» She is shifting uncomfortably in her chair. I ask what sensations, feelings or words are emerging. Her voice is quiet but her body is not.

» I feel an inner nudge within myself to stand up and move closer to her. Before doing so, I ask Jill for her permission. She agrees. I rise and stand next to her, looking downward at her sitting in the chair. Her eyes grow wider.

» With rising momentum, Jill jumps to her feet with a clear booming voice yelling "ASSHOLE!" She's startled by her own voice and volume. I reassure her that it's okay to express at this volume. Her face forms a sheepish smile. Jill then begins to repeat the ASSHOLE word several times, each time louder and with a nervous laugh in between.

» Jill's expression of anger now trails back down into a core sensation held in her stomach area which she is now touching with both hands.

» Jill's laughter begins to turn into tears and she sits back down. I encourage her to feel her bodily sadness and she allows herself to sob. Several more minutes pass. I help her to hold a safe space for her deep, deep sadness to be felt, understood and then released.

» Jill then begins to talk about her narcissistic mother. She passed away last year. Jill spoke about how she was often made to feel invisible by her mother. Jill was now able to connect how her relationship with mother was similar to what she felt with her co-worker.

In a follow-up session we investigated Jill's current beliefs about anger. We explored what she thinks about people who become angry. Again, she talked about her mother who often had angry tirades. As a child, Jill became frightened and paralyzed by her mother's explosions. She learned to suppress anger and other emotions that resembled anything remotely like her out-of-control mother.

Today, Jill is choosing a new pro-aging belief about her emotions, including anger. She is learning to honor a wider range of feelings in her life. It's no accident that Jill has also found it easier to detach from her co-worker's self-centered ways.

Attitudinal Alchemy

Originally, the science of alchemy was about turning lead into gold. Modern day alchemy involves taking the energy of consciousness and turning it into transformation. In the early 1980's, I first met a true modern alchemist and healer. Her name is Louise Hay. As synchronicity would have it, we turned out to be next door neighbors while living in the Santa Monica, CA area. At the time, she was working with individuals medically diagnosed with AIDS. Understandably, many were grief stricken and locked in daily terror. I would stop over at Louise's home and watch her turn lead into gold.

First hand, I witnessed Louise teach men and women of all ages how to release their self-defeating attitudes. She helped them unplug from the social stigmas brought on by a mean homophobic culture. Louise knew that even if some were not physically cured, all of them were in the midst of attitudinal healing. In particular, I remember one young man who was preparing to leave his body. He became busy filling his heart with forgiveness and more life appreciation. Later, I heard his transition out of this life was peacefully seamless.

Are you experiencing hardening of the attitudes? Where is it showing up?

Our Bodies Speak For Us

Our body is a biofeedback system for what attitudes we continue to hold, both conscious and unconscious. The body will always tells us what our minds are simply not ready to acknowledge. As we age, poor health does not just randomly descend on us. When we deny the intelligence and feedback of the human system, we are choosing to believe that illness just happens out of the blue. Simply put, our body responds to what we feed it. Often, our current health status is a mirror of our loyalty to certain repetitive beliefs. These thoughts may be known or unknown to you.

In particular, our wise human body holds emotional, physical and psychic trauma until one is ready to face it and release it. I'm a big fan of asking the body what it needs. No matter what condition of health you're in, write a letter to your body and let it respond back to you. Create a dialogue in your journal between you and your body. Explore your writings and include your reflections about your night-time dreams (priceless free therapy). How is your body speaking for you today? If you listen, it will show you what it needs. Stay conscious and it will also supply you with your specific healing protocol.

Pro-aging doesn't mean we never get ill. It means we seek to understand how our thoughts and feelings and environment may be contributing to one's compromised health. If you readily accept only conventional medical labels for an illness, you restrict your capability to fully self-heal.

Through my professional years, I've witnessed many individuals who gave up their own common sense and their innate healing power in favor of placing all their decision-making into the hands of their medical doctors. This type of abdication reminds me of the influences that sprouted in the Middle (Dark) Ages. This was after the decline of the Roman Empire when a heavy chain of patriarchal-religious factions ruled. These "religious figures" convinced the masses they had to repeatedly go through a holy intermediary (them) in order to experience God. Middle men still make me nervous. The truth is that medical doctors are just human beings. If you receive an uncomfortable diagnosis, make sure you seek at least two other health practitioner opinions, including from a qualified naturopath, chiropractor or acupuncturist. Pro-ager's learn to never abdicate their innate healing power.

We've got our work cut out for us as we rescue ourselves from increased medicalization and confront the stereotypes that feed the decline model of aging, i.e. "everything is downhill from here." In the United States, our so-called healthcare institutions are run by fear. One huge arena in which this fear is played out is with pharmaceutical advertising. Big Pharma companies love it when we diagnose ourselves with one more deficiency and then run to a doctor for confirmation—and a prescription. Pharmaceutical corporations will do anything to kill the message of self-healing in order to grow their stock prices. In America, we could take a conscious lesson from our global neighbors. Many European countries continue to ban pharmaceutical propaganda from entering their living spaces through T.V. and other media screens.

I'm not suggesting that anyone should forego all medications, medical advice or treatments. In fact, when needed, please avail yourself of modern medicine. It can be beneficial and life-saving. When you do need to approach the medical system, however, I'd suggest you utilize the **pro-aging medical motto: *never go in alone!*** Take a healthy pro-aging buddy with you who can help you maneuver through the medical maze. Their job is to keep reminding you what is still working well and the reality of your own self-healing capacity. Think about this: We have 50-70 trillion working cells in our body at all times. Do you really want to believe that you're broken?

Energy Cardiology

For thousands of years, acupuncturists have long understood that "the Heart is the Emperor". As the saying goes, what's good for the heart is good for the being.

Biologically, we know that the heart emits significant fields of sound, pressure waves, light and electrical-magnetic signals which impact all cells in the body at various times and rhythms. The Institute of HeartMath (www.heartmath.org) research reveals that the heart has its own intrinsic nervous system independent of the brain. In their labs, participants were shown emotionally evocative images and their heart carrier waves were monitored. Pictures that evoked fear, anger or sadness created incoherent rhythms within the body. In contrast, when participants were shown pictures that evoked care, love and compassion, their heart carrier waves were smoothly coherent. What they discovered is that the heart receives the information *first* and then relays it to the brain, which then goes to the rest of the body.

Here's what they weren't prepared for: Even *before* each picture was shown, the participant's physiology responded, and the first responder was the heart. In other words, the heart is intuitive and can recognize what's already in the field.

Our heart-brain-body has access to a field of information not bound my time and space. In quantum physics, this is very old news. Simply put, we are an electrical-vibrational system connected to larger grids of energy, light and information. In my practice, I often refer to the work of Dr. Eric Pearl—Reconnective Healing® and author of *The Reconnection: Heal Others, Heal Yourself.* In my experience, it is upgraded type of energy medicine that provides a full spectrum of healing.

When illness is present, it causes density, heaviness or slower vibrations in our physical body and our energy field (also called the *subtle energy body*). If you treat the emotional and the energetic components to your illness, your physical body will benefit. As mentioned, we each possess a natural intelligence and have the ability to gain access to one's inner apothecary. Self-healing does not imply flying solo. If you're feeling compromised by your mental and physical aspects, locate a trained healer or attend a qualified group that can help you tap into your own inner healer.

Starting in my early twenties, I've consistently sought out and have been helped by those who utilize self-healing principles. I've always been fascinated with evolving structures that have been created for the purpose of increased well-being. In my own life, I meet regularly (often weekly) with a small group of remarkable women. One life-saving tool that has emerged from our pro-aging circle has been an increased understanding of *life energy management*.

To master one's life energy, begin with your emotional self. Powerful early experiences that are unresolved, may express themselves years later, often through physical symptoms or even serious illness. In order to understand the purpose of a particular health-related condition or situation, start with your emotions. Denial means that you're pretending that you're not feeling something. Like the lottery, you have to be in it to win it. Each of your emotions holds a unique energetic frequency. Women, typically, have fuller access to a wider range of these emotional frequencies. Therefore, all the more reason for you to have an emotional-processing method at your disposal.

Unfinished Business

We all have it. In the previous chapter I suggested that you make a list of your regrets, resentments and any other unfinished business. **Healthy pro-aging requires cleaning up our past so we can live more fully in the present.** Just think, you don't have to wait until the very end to see your life flash before you (if indeed that happens). Instead, consciously review your life while you're still alive!

We cannot change the fact that we have harmed others and others have harmed us. The gift of self-healing reminds us to continually sweep our side of the street by taking responsibility for our past and present actions. What are you finding? From working in the trenches, I'm convinced that holding resentments is the quickest way to shave years off one's life.

How do you know if you're still holding resentment towards someone? Here's one litmus test. Let's say you're sitting comfortably in a room and "this person" walks through the doorway. Do you instantly want to flee? Do you begin to feel sick to your stomach? Do you feel your blood pressure rising through the roof? If so, chances are Mr. or Ms. X still belongs on your grudge list. Holding on to resentment is similar to taking the hemlock poison and expecting the other person to die. Who's still on your grudge list and for what reasons?

The Pride Factor

When we struggle to forgive someone, what we are really struggling with is our own pride. Let go of pride and forgiveness will come more easily. Every day's an opportunity to let go of another sliver of false pride that keeps one locked in the past. Here's a true story from my own life.

A couple months after my father passed, I volunteered to help out at a special event. Clearly, I was not on my best game and I ended up making more mistakes with personnel, than usual. The woman overseeing my volunteer area was very upset with me. I apologized to her for my errors and mentioned my grieving state. Unfortunately, she was not able to leave it at that. After the event, she proceeded to send out an email broadcast to others in our volunteer circle, about my incompetency. While not wanting to engage in her criticism, I still allowed her actions to really hurt me. It was difficult for me to forgive her. In fact, my pride factor didn't allow it.

A few months later, I discovered God's roulette table was in full action. After a weeklong international conference, my life partner—Jim and I boarded a huge Airbus commercial jet for a thirteen hour flight back to Los Angeles. When I came down the aisle, guess who was sitting in the assigned seat right next to me? You're right—that uncompassionate woman! I quickly excused myself and walked directly to the back of the plane. Frantically, I began looking for a couple empty seats together. I would have settled for one. There were none. It was clear that I had to fully grasp the odds of this cosmic set-up. So for the next ten minutes, I squeezed myself into the tiny airplane bathroom to curse, cry and eventually...surrender.

Staring back at me in that bathroom mirror was a reflection of my own pride, perfectionism and lack of compassion. Standing next to the tiny toilet, I humbly asked my Creator to heal me and this relationship. Squeezing myself out through the folding bathroom door, I began that long journey back to my assigned seat. Interestingly, my heart began to open wider with each passing row of that filled-to-capacity jumbo jet. By the time I reached my assigned seat, I knew that God had healed something in me that I could not have done by myself.

As a result, this woman and I were able to have some kind interchanges. There was no talk about the past nor were any apologies exchanged. We stayed present with one another and it was sufficient to my open heart. What was my learning? Sometimes, the gift of Self-Healing has to come and hunt us down.

Accepting the truth of someone's limitations will help you to forgive. Hurtful acts are a display of woundedness. As the saying goes, *hurting people hurt other people.* Forgiveness allows us to empty ourselves of these old scripts we keep repeating. They are often reactive and protective judgments to keep the ego justified in "being right" which often translates to making the other person "totally wrong". Our black and white thinking is just a product of the limited mind.

Would you like more peace in your life? Ask your Higher Power for assistance. You have nothing to lose but a state of mind that has killed off many moments of serenity. If you haven't done so already, bravely pick up a pen, pencil or fingernail polish and write out your grudge list now.

Bless Them, Change Me

The next step involves making gentle amends to yourself and others. Apologize for your past actions if it will not inflict more injury on others. When making an apology (in person, if possible), don't bring up their part. Allow that to come from them, which may or may not happen. Even if you sincerely apologize for your behavior, the other person may or may not simply forgive you. That's not the point. You're the one that will benefit. Pro-aging is about lightening up the weight of that backpack that you carry around. Don't forget to include yourself in the amends process. When you make direct amends and experience more forgiveness, the heavy rocks of bitterness, sadness, guilt and self-hatred can and will fall away. But don't just take my word, see for yourself.

Forgiveness is an ongoing practice. It's rarely a onetime event. The ability to love without conditions is perhaps the most difficult of all feats. **Research is on your side: as you age forgiveness tends to happen more easily**. Stay focused with completing this important pro-aging task. If it helps, employ one of my favorite sayings, *bless them, change me*. As you continue to tuck in your ego pride and make amends to those on your grudge list, periodically check in with a pro-aging buddy about your progress and timeline.

The Gift of Vulnerability

Journal entry—July 2011

My 82- year-old father had been diagnosed with advanced stage melanoma cancer.

Emotions are flaring—his, mine, brother, sister and other family members. Disease is such a tricky road to maneuver through. Rawness abounds. He's 82 and filled with so much anxiety. I want so much to fix him. It appears the best medicine that I can offer him is my time and love. I've decided to go back to Wisconsin and be with him. My mind is frightened. How will I do this? How can I help Dad and take care of myself? What unfinished business do we have? How can I afford this? What about my clients?

One more time, I turn to Source for answers. I'm reminded that I'm not in charge of when Dad will leave his body. Dad mirrors the inevitability of my future—my mortality, my own death. On this topic, I once heard Prem Rawat say, "Were all in that same line, some of us are just further up in the queue". Yes, it's true; we all share the same vulnerability. All I know is that I must go back to hug him. It's time to go be with my Poppa.

Capital DEATH

Facing our mortality is equally as important as recognizing our immortality. Jungian analyst, Albert Kreinheder describes what he calls the preparation for 'capital DEATH'. He goes on to explain, "One of the serious conditions that older people often have is death anxiety. This is a real killer, a self-fulfilling prophecy. Paradoxically those who want to live well have to learn to die well." Kreinheder tells the story of a popular Jungian analyst. Starting at age 35, this San Francisco analyst reported that a day didn't go by that he didn't think about his own death. The popular analyst-therapist was full of life and well known for his energy and vitality despite his own daily death thoughts. Ironically, the analyst didn't pass away until he was in his 90's. The story goes that when his time did come, he died peacefully. But then again, he had a very long time to prepare.

How do we prep for our own capital DEATH? Gilda Franz, the author of *Being Ageless: The Very Soul of Beauty* writes "if we don't prepare for old age, we feel raped by it." Aging and death is like a journey to a foreign land, and like any other trip, one wonders what to pack.

For me, it comes down to lots of love. In the eleventh century, poet-teacher Rumi, knew what to pack on his journey when he wrote, **"Through love all pain will turn to medicine".** What do you want to pack? My pro-aging suggestion is to take a lover with you. But don't just choose anyone. Pick the attentive lover that has already brilliantly done its packing. This lover awaits in your own heart filled with comfort and understanding.

Each moment we live on the cusp of mortality and immortality. We have been graciously created from the elements of life that are both temporary and permanent. This is how it is. The longer we stay in this human body, our skin becomes more transparent and so must we. In particular, crying is an instinctual and natural balancing release for this precious human ecosystem. Tears remove toxins. Even tears of joy can be a magnificent way to detox. Like sweating, crying is the body's wise attempt to cool and clear itself.

Self-Healing—Six Questions

Take a moment and answer the following:

1. Do you allow your tears and other vulnerable emotions to surface?
2. Do you override your emotions with more caffeine, sugar, excessive work or exercise, over-volunteering, shopping, TV, or getting too involved in other people's drama?
3. What are some of your other favorite distractions?
4. What vulnerable emotions do you tend to avoid feeling?
5. Who do you reach out to (or need to) for help with your transparency and healing?
6. What feelings arise when you think about your own 'capital DEATH'?

Working "8 to Faint"

A *Washington Post* report revealed some important, yet surprising feedback from Baby Boomers. Many of us appear to be less healthy than our ancestors were at the same age. In spite of gym memberships, many Boomers are less physically active than their parents and grandparents. This is due in part to longer hours on the freeway and jobs that keep us in front of a computer screen all day.

Although there are fewer smokers in our generation, more Boomers are likely to report chronic pain, drinking, psychiatric problems, high blood pressure, high cholesterol and debilitating levels of stress. And that's the short list. The rising stats on women over forty are showing growing percentages of alcohol dependency, food addiction, workaholism, shopping addictions and prescription drug abuse. What is your body saying about an "8 to Faint" schedule?

In her timely book, *The Baby Boomer Diet,* Donna Gates describes how we easily turn to "Quick-fix solutions—cosmetic procedures, anti-aging hormones, and extreme diets to stave off the aging process. But these methods are akin to repainting a dilapidated car. At first glance, these cosmetic changes may improve the appearance, but they don't account for more important and deep-seated issues. These can only be addressed through an understanding of our inner ecosystem; and how diet, food purity and selection, and lifestyle choices can lessen the effects of aging, giving us not just longer lives, but better ones."

Boomers must confront new and often premature health threats simply because of the world we've been living in. Our bodies were not designed to absorb synthetic chemicals throughout an entire lifetime, even in small doses. Environmental toxins damage our immune systems. They increase our predisposition to illness and disease. Environmental toxins have proven to be altering our DNA. From the moment sperm and egg cells come together, toxins have been found to be already present. These toxins are being passed on through the umbilical cord and blood of the mother, to our children and generations to come.

To make matters worse, Boomers are particularly vulnerable to age discrimination in this shaky global economy. We are often among the first to be laid off and the last to be rehired by employers who perceive us as more expensive and less flexible than younger workers. According to recent AARP statistics, the unemployment rate for those 55+ has jumped 103% since the December 2007 recession began.

Once again, our generation is faced with redefining itself. For many, this literally has meant starting over. Faulty pension plans or no savings at all, rising life expectancy and aging parents, means many will need to work much longer than our parents ever did, whether we want to or not.

> **Remember when teachers, public employees, Planned Parenthood, NPR & PBS crashed the stock market, wiped out half of our 401K's, took trillions in taxpayer funded bail outs, spilled oil in the Gulf of Mexico, gave themselves billions in bonuses, and paid no taxes?**
>
> **Yeah, me neither...Pass it on.**
>
> (Sent to me by a Wisconsin School Psychologist & Union Activist)

The Good News

Some things are meant to be simple. The gift of self-healing means that we quench our fundamental needs. What are the basic building blocks that we require? Each human being needs plentiful access to clean water, pure food, safe shelter, caring connection with others and daily contentment. The good news is that our planet already possesses enough resources for each human being to be fed inside and out. The issue at hand is reducing greed and increasing distribution. Pro-aging involves a noble mission to self-heal, feel good, and whenever possible help disperse the plenty.

Feeling inner contentment is not a luxury—it is a basic human fundamental need. When one uncovers the thirst of their timeless heart something wonderful happens. Personal peace is possible. That's been my ongoing experience for many years now. You can learn more about the journey of joy from Prem Rawat at www. premrawat.com.

What else is essential? Never underestimate the power of sleep. As a child, I remember hearing my parents or grandparents ramble on when they experienced a particular good night of sleep. Now I fully understand them. Dr. Craig Heller and his team at Yale University, study what he calls a growing "National Sleep Deficit." They study the many consequences of shortened or disrupted sleep. Dr. Heller lists the accounts of medical mistakes and large-scale disasters that most likely have occurred due to sleep deprivation. Healthy pro-ager's recognize the value of a consistent bedtime schedule and learn to guard their nightly sleep cycle like a precious jewel.

In the USA, we are productivity-obsessed and so many find it difficult to rest when the body is tired. (OK, I admit, cat naps are still new to me too). I work with clients and colleagues, addicted to daily grande lattes, skipping their meals and wonder why they need sleeping pills each evening. If my office walls could talk you'd hear my voice emphatically say: *"Feeding caffeine to your already exhausted adrenal glands is like whipping a tired horse. It's cruel and insane!"*

Many Boomer women are seeking relief from exhaustion and over-responsibility. Despite one's fatigue, many women continue to distract and deplete themselves in the name of "helping others". Often, the ones they are allegedly "helping" are actually very capable adult human beings (who can help themselves). Yes, I know it is not easy to hang up the Super-Woman cape. If you've run out the clock out on being wired, tired and expired— thank you for admitting it. I'll elaborate more on this weighty topic in Chapter Three.

> **Definition of maturity**
>
> *Bing Dictionary*
>
> Mature state: the condition of being ripe, fully aged, or fully grown, especially mentally or emotionally.

Stuck in a Developmental Cul-de-sac

No one arrives into mature adulthood in one piece. Aspects of our personality can get stuck, while other parts grow and thrive into full maturity. These maturity gaps are often due to earlier conditioning. Many people have a discrepancy between their chronological age and their developmental age. Active symptoms of depression, anxiety and addictions can mask our immature parts. Most of us grown-ups still need to mature in some area(s) of our life.

Be careful now, are you thinking about someone else who needs to grow up? If so, gently bring the focus back to your own side of the pro-aging fence. **What repeated stressor is showing up in your life that's possibly due to a lag in maturity?**

My own maturity gap showed up repeatedly in my earnings and work life. Here's a little more background. Growing up on a large dairy farm, my physical work-life started quite young and remained labor intensive. My child-adolescent self encoded the physiology of work, work, and more work. You can't argue with generations of cellular memories filled with hard physical farm labor. Playtime didn't usually happen until the cows were milked, the pigs, sheep, horses, cats and dogs were all fed and the fifty pound hay bales were successfully stacked in the hay mow. Farm and house chores were daily and by no means trivial. By the time I reached the age of sixteen, I felt I had completed enough physical work for several lifetimes.

Like many teens, I wanted to be any place but home (especially not at the farm). On the outside, I pretended to be self-sufficient and mature, but inside I wasn't. In my senior year of high school, devastating losses were hitting my family. My father's depression worsened. My mother left him for a much younger, attentive lover. During my parents' divorce, my father was in a psychiatric hospital for months. It was the mid-70's, and his depression treatment was heavy sedative drugs and twenty-eight rounds of electric shock treatments. Our six generation family farm and hundreds of acres of land ended up on the auction block. Within a few months of each other, both of my paternal grandparents died from cancer.

Heavy losses continued during my first year of college. I put up a stiff upper lip but inside I had collapsed. By the time I graduated from college (with honors, of course), all my suck-it-up muscles were ready for a break.

My secret rescue plan was to find a nice, wealthy, good-looking man to take care of me. The paradox was that I had been raised in a semi-liberal household where feminism was encouraged. California sounded like a great place to go live and figure out my quandary. In 1980, shortly after arriving at U.C. Berkeley (where else) and trying to cope with my past, I hit a bottom with my own unresolved pain and addictions.

Thankfully, within months of my California arrival, I was able to ask for help and begin my recovery process. As you probably guessed, the white-knight-rescue thing didn't pan out so well. I had to learn to grow up, re-parent myself and become the rescuer that I was looking for.

Today, I pay close attention to my inner teen. If I don't, she screams very loudly (as teenagers do so well). My inner teen keeps a watchful eye on my work-load commitments. She reminds me: *Enough of the farm-girl work mentality. This girl just wants to have fun!* With her ongoing input, I continue to refine my work, money and playtime responsibilities. With ongoing awareness, I'm less blinded by old money messages and outdated workaholic beliefs. Today, I choose improved thoughts and actions that support my life energy and feed my financial maturity.

The Biology of Hope

It's common knowledge that chronic stressors depress our immune system. Science confirms that joy and laughter feed our immune cells. **A recent University of California-Irvine research study shows that even looking forward to a good laugh can stimulate a healthy immune response.** This is the first evidence-based study to prove that *anticipating* a funny movie or a positive event can be good for our health.

What fun-filled experience are you anticipating?

The Messenger

Way before the big psychology buzz with neuroscience research, I was fortunate to be trained in body-mind healing alongside some phenomenal chiropractors, naturopaths and acupuncturists. They taught me to explore "beyond the talking head" in the therapy room. What is the physiological basis of body-mind based healing?

The answer: neuropeptides. Every thought you think and every emotion you feel, communicates to each cell in your body. How? It is done courtesy of tiny protein molecules called neuropeptides. Each cell in your body has receptor sites to receive these messages from our thoughts, emotions and behaviors. Our entire physiology is connected to our nervous system via this incredible neuropeptides system.

What messages about aging are we feeding our neuropeptides? According to current mainstream American media-advertisements, here are the top five negative adjectives that describe our aging milieu: *slow, weak, timid, forgetful and unfashionable.* No wonder we keep thinking that growing old is pitiful.

As Lauren Kessler describes in *Counter Clockwise: My Year of Hypnosis, Hormones, Dark Chocolate, and Other Adventures in the World of Anti-Aging,* "After years of hearing jokes about being over-the-hill at 40 or 50 or 60, after seeing thousands of commercials for Depends and Ensure and cell phone keypads with three-inch high numerals, after watching hundreds of movies and television shows with cranky, crabby, asexual older people, suppose you begin to conflate "old" with sick, debilitated and diminished?"

Do you think old is bad? I did and sometimes still do. That's why I had to write this book and you are choosing to read it. In an anti-aging culture that doesn't honor maturity, we all need more hope. On this important note, according to a Yale University study, the perceptions a person held about aging had more impact on how long he or she lived than did their cholesterol level, blood pressure, or whether they were smokers. Regardless of age, gender, socioeconomic status, loneliness, or the actual state of their health, **the men and women with positive views on aging lived seven and a half years longer than those who bought into the negative stereotypes.**

The bottom line: Self-healing is learning to feed your neuropeptides a more positive message about being alive. Unconditional love is the best medicine we can receive and dispense.

Blue Zones: People Who Live the Longest

Blue Zones: Lessons for Living Longer from the People Who've Lived the Longest
National Geographic- Dan Buettner (2008)—www.bluezones.com

The best strategies for longevity were found in what is called "Blue Zones".

The people living there share four main traits;

> » They eat a healthy, plant-based diet
>
> » Live an active lifestyle
>
> » Have a clear sense of purpose
>
> » Develop strong social networks

CHAPTER THREE

The Gift of Discernment

"Is It Your Burger to Flip?"
—SISTER B

I was in my early twenties when Melody Beattie first dropped the "C" bomb. *Codependent No More,* the book and recovery movement has helped changed the lives of millions. It certainly shed a spot light on my own childhood coping skills. I felt and acted as the "over-responsible one" for pretty much everything and everyone. I took great pride in "cheering people up". As I've learned, all this need for "helping" was my way of trying to control the uncontrollable.

Feeding Time at the Human Zoo

At the grill of life, we've each been given a burger. Most women feel compelled to watch and flip other people's burgers, even at the expense of burning themselves. By midlife, it's not easy to learn how to flip one's own burger and then step away from the grill. Here's an important pro-aging point (which I know you already know). *It's always feeding time at the human zoo!* **If you're feeling drained at the grill of life, ask yourself this key question: Is it really my burger to flip?**

One definition of **discernment** *is the act of exhibiting keen insight and good judgment.* As time and gravity continue to have their way, where are you putting your focus? Besse Cooper, the world's oldest living person on record from the peach state of Georgia, who lived to celebrate her 116th birthday spoke about her focus. When interviewed by Guinness World Records she said "I mind my own business and I don't eat junk food". God bless you, Besse.

Baby Boomers love to stay busy in this human zoo—so many cages to visit. After all, we're in the middle of what has been termed our "sandwich generation years". On one slice of life, we have the needs of parents who are living longer and may require more assistance. Today, there are almost 6 million Americans age 85 or over. By 2040, the number will have shot up to more than 14 million, according to U.S. Census projections. That means a lot of eldercare in our future—including the search for more lost keys, picking up prescriptions and sitting by hospital beds.

The other side of the Boomer sandwich may involve trying to launch grown children and/or step-children into a struggling economic world. U.S. statistics show more adult children are NOT leaving home while many more are returning back to home base. While others of you may have a heaping plate filled with a special needs child (who may never leave home) or you're caretaking an ill partner/ spouse. In the middle of this people sandwich what's a busy, stressed and over-responsible woman to do? Receive the gift of discernment.

When is it Your Time?

Maybe you still have adult children living with you or they fled the nest and now have returned to roost with you. Economic factors including reduced available jobs, tuition debt and rising living costs drive many college graduates back home. Often called the 'Boomerang Generation', according to CBS News a record 15 million young adults have entered parental living arrangements. Though common in many other countries, multi-generational families are an increasing trend in the United States. If you have a fledgling adult who has landed on your doorstep, be prepared to employ the gift of discernment. Your sanity is completely on the line here. Here's a question on the topic from one of my blog readers, followed by my emphatic response.

Q. *My 24-year-old son has moved back home, he is our youngest child. I was just getting used to not having to pick up after everyone's messes. I don't want to come down hard on him because he's had a rough go of it this past year with finishing college. He's not been able to find a job. I'm trying not to feel so agitated about his lackadaisical behaviors. It's been 7 months since he's moved home. What should I do about this?*

A. Listen to your agitation. It's telling you something is not working. **Codependents don't have relationships, they have situationships.** Please take a pause and think about that statement. Now say this out loud: *My breast feeding days are over.* Yes, it is time to close the nursery. This is your opportunity to upgrade your boundaries with your grown son. Please repeat it with me and this time with more gusto... *MY BREAST FEEDING DAYS ARE OVER!!!*

A key indicator of codependency is that we repeatedly do things for others who are fully capable to do these things without us. Does this apply to your situation with your son or others? If so, I'd suggest you go online or visit your nearest bookstore or library to obtain one of many helpful books on codependency recovery. Some other key words include: *enabling, entitlement, people pleasing and jumbo shrimp.* Yes, I know that last one was pretty random but I'm just checking to see if you're still with me.

Teach your son how to treat you. Respect your own grown-up resources that you've worked hard to gather. Your home needs to be an oasis for you and your spouse. For the time being, your son is a temporary guest.

Understandably, these are challenging work times for Americans of all ages. Since your son has been having a rough go of it, maybe it's time he (or you) seek some professional assistance? For everyone's sake, it's important to know if his 'lackadaisical behaviors' are related to a mental illness or any abusive usage patterns with alcohol, drugs, food, online gaming, gambling or sex. If you suspect or find evidence that he is involved with mood altering substances or unhealthy activities, I suggest you obtain help from a professional trained in addictions and family systems. I'd also suggest you attend some Codependency Anonymous or Al-Anon meetings. Look online for local face-to-face meetings or telephone meetings. Give yourself at least six different meetings to see if it speaks to you and your situation in some helpful way. There is one other very important action step.

Write up a Written Contract for adult children living at home. Whether his/her stay is due to convenience, mental illness or financial hardship, your relationship has now changed. Your adult child needs to learn how to act like an adult in your home. This means adhering to your house rules, contributing financially when able, and showing respect to you and any other person living in or visiting your home.

If your adult child has no income source at this time and is job hunting, allow him/her to work off rental obligations by performing maintenance work, extra cleaning or other tasks that you deem helpful. Make and sign a written contract so that you and your adult child's responsibilities and expectations are crystal clear. I can't emphasize enough how a written contract has saved many of my clients and their families from the ongoing drama of entitlement, vagueness, and chaos. If you'd like a free detailed sample of a written contract, visit my website at: *www. marcianewman.com/adultchildrencontract*

> **Just because you have a uterus and breasts does not mean you are biologically designed to do grocery shopping.**
>
> **—Christine Northrup, M.D.**

Mind Your Own Business

When caught up in what others are doing or not doing, we lose the gift of discernment. Humility goes out the door. Benjamin Franklin cleverly wrote "Clean your finger before you point at my spots." Clearly, our contribution to humanity increases when we allow others to be exactly as they are. Or as global speaker Prem Rawat has reminded many audiences, "Hey, let's just give each other a little bit more elbow room, okay?"

Rule of thumb: If your thoughts begin with "he should" or "she should" you've entered the twilight zone of codependency. For instance, my own inner Empress loves to play the Queen of Everything. Sometimes, she truly believes the Creator deemed her (me) the Ruler of appropriate social behaviors, good business conduct and highway courtesy. *Yikes.*

Both anti-aging thinking and co-dependent thinking are rooted in fear. This unprocessed fear creates an ongoing nagging sensation of lack. The more marginalized and diminished one feels in this world (a common theme in growing older), the greater the opportunity to make friends with our "approval seeker". This is the deeper processing work of creating healthy pro-aging.

If need be, take a well-deserved short break, then come back and answer the following **Mind Your Own Business—Three Questions**. In doing so, you'll be gifting yourself a life-saving tool called healthy detachment. Contact your pro-aging buddy to hear your responses and your new healthier commitments.

1. If I wasn't so busy trying to manage so and so's life (and/or feeding somebody else's vision) what could I focus on in my own life?

2. What other over-responsible activities (control things) do I do?

3. Which one(s) am I willing to let go of? When?

Carry-Over Behaviors

For thousands of years, our female ancestors engaged in supporting the visions of others, typically husbands and more recently—male bosses. Even today, most women produce some type of guilt when launching their own projects. It's as if the female DNA helix has been embedded with a primal code: *the care of others must always come before one's own needs.*

Putting the focus back on managing your own mid-life requires chutzpah. Those around you may have to flounder for a bit. Let them. When you release these carry-over (caretaking) behaviors, waves of guilt and fear will come to the surface. Remember, to use a processing method to recognize, feel and release them. Know that these constricting thoughts and feelings are not who you really are. Let them pass through your body-mind.

To live an authentic life means that you will continue to upset others. Healthy pro-ager's live with the reality that some people will never like us and certain people will always be disappointed (usually family members). When faced with not measuring up to other people's expectations, I have a wise feminine friend who replies with a healthy *"Oh well"*.

In current female development research, it's a well-known fact that many young girls often lose their voice by the age of ten. For most Boomer women, the odds are that it happened much younger. As little girls growing up in the 1950's, any loud or opinionated voices were bombarded and re-shaped with these messages; *Be sugar and spice and everything nice. Make sure you look pretty so xxx will like you. Be seen and not heard. Play nice and don't speak so loudly so others will want to play with you.* What happens to hyper-verbal little girls who don't want to play by those ridiculous and silencing adult rules? Here's a bit of my own story about that.

My frustrated rural elementary school teachers didn't know what to do with me at times. I enjoyed leading mini-revolts against these idiotic girl rules. Starting from a young age, I could sense many things including my grade school teacher's insecurities. Early on, I didn't play 'teacher's pet' since I knew that trying to make them feel better didn't feel good to me. Most of all, I didn't like many of their silly rules, so I questioned them. Understandably, they just wanted me to be quiet and not influence my peers so much.

Unfortunately, one unhappy twisted teacher actually duct-taped my mouth and marched me out into the school hallway. This person shoved me into an outside corridor where other classes of students and teachers passed by and practiced their rubber-necking skills. Hours dragged by (so it seemed) as I sustained the hallway of shame. Remarkably, I learned how to survive my elementary school inquisition.

My voice went underground for awhile until it would surface again. Then a school authority would swoop down at me like a SWAT team, targeting me with their bullets of disapproving looks and school detentions. At least their message was consistent; WE KNOW MORE THAN YOU, SO WE'LL PUT YOU BACK INTO YOUR PLACE.

On my journey of self-respect I have come to learn the following: When others don't feel in charge of their own lives, they may try to take charge of yours. Don't let them. Shield yourself with the strength of your own discernment and self-worth. Carol Osborn, author of *Fierce With Age,* speaks out that "Boomer women apologize way too much". In fact, she created a personal list of those things she commits to no longer needing to apologize for. Go ahead and have fun by creating your own list: Things I Will No Longer Apologize For!

Another ancient carry-over behavior for women is the need to prove (over and over again) that our voices and visions are worthy enough. In novelist Anna Quindlen's recent memoir, *Lots of Candles, Plenty of Cake,* she writes, "We all needed to be more than we already were. But more was never enough. The best thing that you can say about this nonsense is that at a certain age we learn to see right through it, and that age is now. I'm not buying the idea that we need to be more, given how much we already are. By the standards that matter—of friendship and diligence and support and loyalty—we are scoring in the top stanine."

Carry-over behaviors dissolve when we replace them with self-acknowledgement behaviors. Healthy discernment is recognizing our wholeness not our deficiencies. Are you interested in more empowerment? Then take out your journal and respond to the following **Carry-over Behaviors-Three Questions**.

1. Do you feel compelled to defend, justify or re-prove your ideas, choices and actions to certain others?

2. To whom and in what situations do you tend give away your power?

3. What are three self-affirming action steps you can take to replace your limiting thinking and behavior?

The Wall

A memorial service was being held in a small town funeral home for a man who had just passed away. The widow had spent over 50 years in a troubled marriage with this man. At the end of the service, the family pallbearers were carrying out the deceased. They accidentally bumped into a wall and shook the wooden casket. Hearing a faint moan, they opened the casket and found out the man was still alive.

For ten more years, the difficult husband lingered on and then one day, suddenly died. The widow held the ceremony at the same funeral home. At the end of the service, as before, the pallbearers begin to carry out the casket.

As they are making their way to the door, this time the widow cries out loudly, **"Watch out for the wall!"**

Healthy Closure Plan

At the present, we remain a culture of death-phobics. How many Vampire-Zombie movies (people who never die), will we have to endure before breaking through our cultural denial about aging and dying? In America, we prefer to send our declining elders to places that we pray that we never end up in. We make our visits brief because it's just too darn confronting.

An anti-aging society neglects the value of humility and so conscious discussions about mortality issues are neglected. We all know that it is important to have clear end-of-life conversations with our partners, spouses, children and parents, but it's uncomfortable—so we put it off. Things like making wills, signing health directives, establishing a cremation or burial fund and fully facing our end-of-life details are often delayed until the crisis hits. If we do proceed, we've been taught to keep these end-of-life discussions hush-hush and behind closed doors. **The gift of discernment invites you and your loved ones to lift these important life tasks out of the shadows.**

In our household, we call it a Healthy Closure Plan. Starting my own end-of-life planning, has been quite eye opening. It sparks the need for more conversations and agreements with my loved ones. My Scorpio sense of humor envisions American women hosting neighborhood "Bucket List / Healthy Closure Parties". Granted, it will be a bit of a departure from a Pampered Chef or a Norwex party.

Healthy Closure Plan—Discussion Questions

Typically, there's no pre-nuptial contract in which one can spell out what tasks one is willing to do (or not do) for their loved ones. Since experts agree that women still end up taking on the bulk of eldercare responsibilities, I encourage you to review and discuss the following with your loved ones, while you're still alive and well.

1. What do you feel you owe your parents?

2. What are you willing to do (or not do) for them?

3. Will you provide them financial support, attend medical appointments with them, allow parents to live with you, etc.?

4. Speak with your parents and find out what they want in terms of eldercare and encourage them to create a Healthy Closure Plan.

5. Do YOU have a will or trust, health directive, a cremation or burial fund and other end-of-life details in place?

6. What do you want/need for your own eldercare?

7. Have you discussed these issues with trusted family members or friends?

8. Have you put your end-of-life requests into a legal document?

If not, meet with your pro-aging buddy promptly. Together, formulate a manageable action plan (with timelines) to gently complete these important closure tasks.

The ART of EXPECTATIONS

Many Boomer women carry unrealistically high expectations of themselves. If left unchecked, such expectations can cause us to develop heightened perfectionism and paralyzing procrastination. When I see these character traits in clients, often this indicates a family history of an absent parent(s). Typically, the absence, abandonment or neglect involved a primary care-taker who 'checked out' through addiction, illness or death. In Julia's case, it began with her mother, a functioning active alcoholic for the first ten years of Julia's life.

> *Ring the bells that still can ring*
> *Forget your perfect offering*
> *There is a crack in everything,*
> *That's how the light gets in.*
> —LEONARD COHEN

I worked with Julia, a bright 49 year-old art gallery owner who was exhausted from working so hard to fill in her cracks of imperfection. She struggled with a compulsive need to look good and have everything in perfect order. She broke into tears as she described writing up an artwork invoice for a prominent Beverly Hills client. Julia was over-the-top horrified that she had made a minor accounting mistake. As she continued to talk, I witnessed self-flagellation taking her hostage. Julia had honed the skill of severely punishing herself. She chastised herself more than any unhappy, customer would. Her unrealistic expectations left her with little self esteem, lots of loneliness and a lack of personal fulfillment. With gentleness we began to focus less on her errors and more on offering herself more compassion as she undertook her re-parenting process.

When we expect ourselves (and others) to be perfect, we withhold love. When we play the perfection card we place ourselves in an ego state of moral superiority. Haven't you noticed how unrealistic expectations lower your life energy? This doesn't mean we abandon our standards and tolerate everything that people throw our way. What it does mean is that we can learn and expect appropriate, realistic and kind human responses starting with ourselves.

In Julia's case, she was able to find her own "good enough mother voice" despite the lack of early bonding with her unavailable biological mother. She continued to make some business mistakes and eventually without such high costs to herself. Julia now understands the difference between humiliation and humility. How much humility do we need? "Just enough to get along with ourselves" as wisely mentioned by Prem Rawat.

Finally, we took Julia's very long list of personal and professional goals and put them into bite-sized action steps. With encouragement, Julia has established a network of supportive friends and re-kindled her connection with certain family members who love her no matter what. She is also now available to give back some unconditional love to them. Julia no longer has to weigh and measure herself by what she perfectly does or doesn't do in this world. She's practicing the art of feeling good—the essence of healthy pro-aging.

The Exertion/Exhaustion Cycle

Boomers love to stay busy. With continued longevity, the gift of discernment invites us to keep taking stock of our gains with clear insight and good judgment. To help us with this, let's briefly look to the central nervous system to more clearly understand the *exertion/exhaustion cycle* that many American women find themselves in.

Up until recently, we've been taught there are two divisions to our autonomic nervous system—the sympathetic and the parasympathetic. The **parasympathetic system** is responsible for producing cell regeneration, relaxation, and digestion. In an overactive state, the parasympathetic can weaken our immune response, produce fatigue, and depression. Similarly, the **sympathetic system,** which prepares us for vigorous physical activity by increasing the heart rate and constricting pupils, can lead to heart problems and severe anxiety when it's active for too long.

When describing the balance of the human nervous system, I often use the simple analogy of an automobile. The sympathetic nervous system is like the accelerator pedal on our car. The parasympathetic nervous system is similar to the brake pedal. When caught in the exertion cycle, you're putting the "pedal to the metal" and forgetting about the brake pedal. Obviously, if you keep doing this you'll eventually run out of gas. When one forgets to properly engage the braking system, exhaustion will surface courtesy of the human body.

Fascinatingly, older neurology research has now been re-visited. It strongly points to a third division in the nervous system—*the enteric which governs the gastrointestinal functions*. Scientists now recognize the web of neurons lining the gastrointestinal tract (stomach, small intestine and large intestine) acts like an independent brain.

In fact, a new field of medicine—*neurogastroenterology* has been created to study it. No doubt, this brings new meaning and scientific back-up to the familiar phrase "listen to your gut instincts".

Your Nervous System Spot Check—Three Questions

1. If my digestive system could talk, what is it saying about my lifestyle right now?

2. What warning signs do I receive when I'm heading for an over-exertion/ exhaustion cycle?

3. In which situations do I need to pump the brake pedal? In which instances do I need to apply the gas pedal more?

Excessive Volunteering

Our Boomer generation is enthusiastically re-inventing the concept of retirement. Even Webster's dictionary definition of *retirement* is now outdated: "to disappear, to go away, to withdraw". Hopefully, more pro-ager's won't see that definition sticking around for long. Whether you are ready to "retire" or not, the gift of discernment invites one to take a closer look at the topic of healthy volunteering.

If you can afford to generously give your time, energy and/or money to people and causes that you believe in, kudos to you. On the other hand, volunteering too much can pose some major problems (just as any excessive work schedule does). I've been there on both counts.

Over a decade ago, my own excessive volunteering led me into an exertion/ exhaustion cycle. I was giving away too much of my time and energy without pay. Don't get me wrong, my heart thoroughly enjoyed the volunteer work. However, over time my body and checkbook revolted. As I came out of my painful denial, I realized how I was not fully taking care of myself— especially on the financial front. For over a year, I was volunteering over 30 hours a week without pay. Needless to say, I had little time and energy leftover to focus on my income producing efforts. In addition, my close relationships and creative projects all fell into the big neglect basket.

All my educational degrees and professional licenses did not teach me how to really value my time, money and life energy. Like many women, we learn about healthy limit setting from the pain of "burn-out". The primary take away of this pro-aging chapter is about building and maintaining better boundaries. No longer do I have to serve humanity while playing the roles of martyr, victim, tyrant or excessive care-taker. I'm learning to employ a higher standard of self-care and this pro-aging guidebook can help you to do that as well. Since I am an imperfect human being, I still have my slips and slides when it comes to boundary setting.

With volunteering, the standard that I try to follow is to offer my services when I'm feeling grateful and rested. I have given myself permission to move away from the concept that helping out means I have to lose or sacrifice something (another carry-over behavior). Feeling content is the highest service I can perform each day. We treat others better when we're happier and healthier. How do you appraise your current level of self care, contentment and volunteer efforts?

> **conversion**
> by Thomas Giles
>
> i converted
> to humanity
>
> last night
>
> simply
> breathing
>
> purest light

The Art of Non-Interference

Discernment is also the ability to let certain aspects of our life alone. Many of us have a compulsive need to fix, analyze or do something. A dear friend reminds me *sometimes the hardest thing to do is nothing*. It takes effort to inhabit present time! Americans love to rush around—as if making more plans makes us feel more important. The ego loves to stay busy and seek out new, shiny distracting objects, people and activities.

One of the joys of growing older is that we can simplify our lives, slow down and have more time to be still. In John O'Donohue's poignant book, *Anam Cara*, (Gaelic for 'soul friend') he wrote, "You will discover that stillness can be a great companion. The fragments of your life will have time to unify, and the places where your soul-shelter is wounded or broken will have time to knit and heal. You will be able to return to yourself. Many people miss out on themselves completely as they journey through life. They know others, they know places, they know skills, they know their work, but tragically, they do not know themselves at all."

An Energy Peel

Many women receive facial peels. How about an energy peel? *A what?*

We live in an unbalanced world of supply and demands. Similar to the physical body, we accumulate waste matter in our mental and energy bodies. Much of our toxic load is from carrying fifty years of other people's stuff (and their agenda's for us). The demands of this outside conditioning can create a heavy, poisonous load over time. Fortunately, we can recognize and learn how to pull out and flush away these accumulated stressors. The solution is called an *Energy Peel*.

Place yourself in an environment of stillness and ask yourself these two questions;

Do I allow enough time and space to come back to myself?

Which people, places and activities deplete me and which of these help to enlighten me?

» Take a moment to look over your calendar for the next three weeks. Remove those people and/or activities that depress and deplete you. Simply excuse your obligatory presence in the name of self-care.

» Create more blank spaces in your schedule for unstructured activity. If you have not created nurturing time and space for yourself in awhile, (or ever), prepare to feel very uncomfortable at first.

» Discover what it feels like to have more unstructured time for things like a spontaneous walk in nature, a replenishing nap, deeper meditation or a hearty belly laugh with a loved one.

» Learn how to contain your inner critic and approval seeker. Compose yourself.

» Let others find their own energy source instead of allowing them to siphon from your tank.

» Keep checking inward. Learn how to feed and stabilize the energy running through your body-mind as easily as you put food into your mouth.

» Pull out your journal and write daily (if possible). Separate your own voice from those of others.

» Sit in the grand silence and ask the Divine to help peel away the accumulated *gunk* (to use a highly technical term).

An energy peel allows you to come back to you. Give yourself the gift of saying "NO" to superficial social functions that rob you of your time, energy and well-being. In your safe environment, establish your own private and sacred guilt-free zone. As you apply more of these chapter suggestions, the gift of discernment will definitely lighten your way. But don't just read or believe my words, complete these pro-aging exercises and see for yourself.

Journal Entry: Come Back to Me

In our soothing green park nearby, I spot a pair of bluebirds. Seeing their presence and bright purple wings in flight are magical to me. My happy just got happier. I find myself being pulled into the children's playground area.

No one else is around. It's just me, the swing set and the slides. The thought comes. "I wonder if my thighs will fit inside that curved swing?" I'm about to find out. Wedging myself into the warm seat, I grasp the metal chains and continue on with the swing set adventure.

Lift off—I'm back in flight! I swing back in time as I remember this movement so vividly. My little one inside has been resurrected. I swing, watch and feel. Shiny luxury cars filled with distracted adults pass by the park.

I return back to this familiar feeling inside of me. This place filled with simplicity, sweet innocence and pleasure. My heart soars as my aching legs pump and pump to sustain a rhythmic swinging motion. Glorious! At one point, I imagine myself on a high trapeze bar.

Enough minutes go by and my head and stomach start to revolt. Crawling out of my wedgy seat, I take with me the Cheshire-cat-smile plastered across my face.

CHAPTER FOUR

The Gift of Wildness

Live in the sunshine, Swim the sea, Drink the wild air.
—Ralph Waldo Emerson

Within each person there is a wild space that is filled with powerful instincts, unbounded creativity and ageless knowing. Though we have been gifted with the Wild woman from birth, our multiple decades of 'civilized living' have muffled her. She has grown silent from over-domestication and too much compliance. The message of pro-aging is calling her back from the endangered species list. The Wild woman will always teach us what it takes to remain raw and real.

Likewise, nature teaches us not by words but by example. There's no intention setting with Mother Nature. She just does her thing and often, quite wildly. Surrounding our home are thousands of acres of preserved native Chumash sacred land, dating back over 12,000 years. During writing breaks, I walk the land and enjoy the variety of visits from our furry and feathery friends. Mother

Nature doesn't tell us how to live. Her un-stoppable ways show us. Mother Nature embodies the Wild woman's mantra: *Don't tell me, show me.*

Honor Your Animal: 101

Hone the art of trusting your animal-ness. Your primal self knows instantly about the environment you've entered and those who inhabit it. In the name of becoming "evolved" we have been trained to over-ride the instantaneous feedback from our ancient primal centers. Our inner animal is keenly aware of who we like and who we don't. Our wild essence constantly monitors our external and internal environments (consciously and unconsciously). If you want to age more comfortably, pay close attention to her.

Feeding your Inner Animal

In what natural environment do you feel most like you are home?

Listen carefully to the response. As soon as you can, make your way to that natural environment and prepare to be fed.

In exchange, leave a gentle and giant footprint of gratitude.

When America was filled with family farms, it was common to be outside together for more hours of the day. We no longer plow the fields together while connecting to the deep fertility of the earth. Instead, we text and tweet each other. We live in cubicles and cars. We exist in the Age of Information and Decision Overload. For example, just go to any large American supermarket and see the stacked shelves of endless choices. Our Wild woman isn't wired to deal with so many choices and all the problem solving. She grows weary with so many electronic devices and hates the commute. Our Wild Woman revolts at having to be so punctual and pleasant all the time. If you allow her the room, she will pull you back to wholeness.

What's a good starting point? Shut off your cell phones and declare a screen-free afternoon for yourself and your loved ones. Then visit a favorite outdoor spot. **Allow your Wild one to unplug and play! Life is bland without her presence.**

To understand the needs of your inner animal in more detail, let's turn to her biological aspects. Research scientist Paul MacLean studied in depth the *primal centers* of the brain. There are three separate and integrated cranial components of what MacLean called 'the triune brain'. Our **reptilian brain** is the most ancient home to our basic protective and survival reflexes. Located in the brain stem and linked to the spinal cord, it mobilizes us to fight, freeze or take flight. If there is trauma and it is too severe, the reptilian brain will immobilize us to shut down or dissociate. This is a protective device of our inner animal. For survival purposes, our reptilian brain will store parts of the trauma until the entire nervous system is more stable and ready to handle it. As a therapist, this is why we often see PTSD (post-traumatic stress disorder) symptoms unravel in layers over an extended period of time in a human lifespan.

The second oldest area of our primal center is our **mammalian brain** which deals with emotions, health, sexuality, and memory storage. It is also been called the limbic system. Our mammalian brain is housed in the following areas; the amygdala, hippocampus, hypothalamus, pituitary gland and thalamus (sensory information). Known as the *brain of relationships,* it also helps your little pet Fido to recognize you from a room full of strangers.

The newest portion of our brain is the **neocortex.** It contains the intellect that we normally associate with thinking and learning. Two for the price of one, our neocortex contains two hemispheres—left and right. Our left frontal brain works with math, logic, reasoning, analysis and words. It is linear, sequential and prefers to tackle details—one thing at a time. Our right frontal brain works with intuition, art, visualization, creativity, spatial relationships, puts information into massive links and prefers to hold the big picture. Our neocortex contains some 100 billion cells, each one of which conducts 1,000 to 10,000 synapses (connections) and has roughly 100 million meters of wiring, all packed into the size and thickness of a formal dinner napkin. Impressive, isn't it?

Both hemispheres are connected through a massive bundle of nerves and tissue called the corpus callosum. Research has shown that the **corpus callosum** is larger in more females, musicians (vs. non-musicians) and in left-handed individuals. Which brings me to a bonus pro-aging dating tip: If you're looking for a partner who's more naturally wired to bring more feeling into present situations, look for the left-handed musicians (been there, done that too). It's also been said that our brain is the most outstanding organ because it works 24 hours a day, 365 days a week— until we fall in love!

At any age, our Wild woman needs to be fed. Even while we celebrate our cerebrocentric victories, the untamed one stirs within. In my own life, she compels me to stroll into the dark night when the great horned owl calls out in a nearby pine tree or when the canyon coyotes begin to howl. I soon recognize the gift of wildness is visiting. Outside, I smile at the bright moon and feel my face and body soften. These nighttime visitors link me to our ancestors who also used to live in trees. Our animal code does not erode, even when we house her in sophisticated concrete structures. Just ask any chiropractor (I happen to live with one) and they'll flash you a full Darwinian smile. They love to point out the remnants of our tails, in the form of that final bone at the end of our spine, called the coccyx.

Udderly Magnificent

OK, I admit it. The truth is, I like to hang with cows. One of my favorite memories from a Nova Scotia vacation involved, yes, watching cows. By now you may know I'm quite familiar with the bovine species. If not, may I emphasize (at least for the Akashic record) that I've logged hundreds of hours of milking them, handled countless hay bales to feed their four stomachs and even assisted with the births of their calves. My lengthy farmer checklist is ad infinitum nauseaum. Let's just say when it comes to cows, "we've met".

Alright, back to my rather tame Canadian cow story. There I was sitting quietly seaside in this North Atlantic pastoral and coastal setting. Nearby, I hear the roar of a tractor approaching, driven by the neighboring farmer. He stops. I see him slowly get off his green steed—a mighty six-wheeled John Deere. He walks over and opens a long wooden gate that leads into an amazing open field, filled with fresh clover. I watch the Holstein cows (those are the black and white ones) carefully watch the farmer. They await the call. He signals them to come. Kicking up their hoofs in a high chorus line fashion, they run immediately towards the farmer. Wildly, yet smoothly they all enter into the newly opened green pasture.

I pause and reflect. "Wow, what if I could trust life like the cows do?" Cows don't seem to stand around questioning the farmer's motives. Can you imagine hearing a herd of worried, cud-chewing heifers complaining *"Where's our next pasture?! Where's our next pasture?! Where's our next pasture?!"* No, they appear to relax and enjoy the one they're already in. And when the farmer does arrive, they are so glad to see him or her. The gentle farmer takes good care of them and for that, they simply trust.

Relational Transparency

Wild women have good reasons for not trusting. Our historical timeline reveals that when the wise feminine became too prominent, these individuals were contained, burned or tortured. For survival purposes, women had to defer again and again to the ruling masculine control and logic. In essence, we've all learned to master the art of serving the intellect. However, without the powerful influence of the feminine, the very heart of mankind became lost. In other words, humanity has tried to grow up without a mother.

Remembrance can serve as a powerful tool for pro-agers. We all have a mutual experience of the feminine. Each one of us spent nine months (give or take) developing inside our biological mother. No matter what kind of relationship we have or had with her, we each hold this cellular memory. We all have been immersed in the unspoken language of the feminine. In the process of being born and living in this world, we forget about this feminine union that is always at our core.

Excitingly, in more places around the world, the power of the feminine is re-emerging. Of course, there will always be pushback from the fundamentalist camps. In America, women's roles have undergone radical changes in the past 125 years (with more to go). For instance, American Boomer women have raised the bar on what relationships and marriage need to deliver. In fact, seventy percent of divorces in the USA are now initiated by females. The number of divorces among those who are 50 years and over has doubled from 1990 to 2010. In mass numbers, Boomer women are opting out of the antique role of being the silent, suffering martyr. Increasingly, American women are no longer willing to be the primary carrier of dissatisfaction in their relationships. **Conscious pro-aging is choosing to NOT to do the emotional work for others in our intimate relationships.**

In today's world, a Wild woman sniffs out a willing partner who can rise to the challenge of being emotionally mature, a good lover and a true companion. With such increased expectations, most twenty-first century couples are clueless how to achieve and sustain relational intimacy in these modern times.

Relational transparency is the ability to be open, communicative, vulnerable and accountable. For almost three decades of being a marriage and family therapist, I see why men's relational evolution in general, has been much slower than women's. This is because of their attachment to the intellect. True intimacy requires vulnerability and healthy women know this. Spot check: **What is your Wild woman saying about your love life?**

The Smart Genie

A husband and wife who each recently celebrated their 60th birthdays were walking on the beach one early evening. As they looked at the water's edge they noticed a colorful bottle. The husband picked it up and rubbed the sand off of it. Instantly, a Genie appeared.

He thanked them for releasing him from the bottle and said he would grant them each a wish.

The Genie turned to the wife and asked for her request. She said "I'd like to help feed the hungry children of the world with all the wealth you give me". *POOF!* The Genie told her to check her Smartphone and she saw there was now 7 Billion Dollars in her bank account.

The Genie then turned to the husband for his wish. The husband quickly replied, "I'd like to make love with a woman that's thirty years younger." The Genie replied "No problem, your wish is my command" and then winked at the wife. *POOF!*

Her husband became 90 years old.

Erotic Intimacy: Bringing it Home

Larry and Carol entered my office with signs of marriage fatigue. Their marriage of 32 years was more than just weary. It was in a semi-comatose state. They were both having sex, just not with each other. Larry, a business owner, began his intrigue with cyberspace sexting and then moved on to physically meeting with another woman. When Carol, a school teacher discovered her husband's affair, she soon followed suit. She did her research by going online to a popular website (for married people who want to have sex with others). She made and kept her appointments for both a wax job and her own fling.

Even with years of working in the relational trenches, I still get surprised when it comes to sex. Larry and Carol represent many mid-life couples (straight or gay). One or both may be freely experimenting sexually outside of their committed relationships, while at home demonstrating puritanical constraint with one other.

To sustain sexual desire within the walls of long-term domesticity takes effort. It's natural that our inner animal revolts at the idea of becoming caged. Let me also be clear. This is not about endorsing or excusing extra-marital affairs. This is not about abdicating one's moral fiber with "my inner animal made me do it". It is, however, about honoring our untamed needs. Esther Perel, one of the most insightful voices on erotic intelligence, emphasizes in her book *Mating in Captivity* that "Desire operates along its own trajectory...sexual desire does not obey the laws that govern peace and contentment between partners."

Hence here is the domestic sex paradox: Couples and families prosper in an environment of comfort and consistency. Eroticism (an aspect of wildness) sprouts from the present moment which is filled with spontaneity, unpredictability and risk. In other words, we are one part domesticated animal and another part that will always possess erotic longing for the wild. Pro-aging is about staying open to our wild one for the long haul and for one's erotic sake.

Our most persistent longings and deepest fears can emerge within the sexual act. How you make love reflects how you have been loved in this life. At birth, you may have had complications or a lack of parent bonding for various reasons, including neglect, trauma or addictions. Yet, the body always remembers what our minds may choose to forget. Perel reminds us that *"the body is our original mother tongue"*. When sharing erotic intimacy, our bodies become a pure, primal tool of expression. It forms a language that does not need words. **Pro-aging is about staying open to**

this human quest for conscious mutuality. Our sexuality and sensuality can be a playground where glorious hedonism and the Divine can collide.

On the topic of sex, let me briefly mention the importance of cinema therapy. It's rare that movies are made about people over fifty, let alone about real life intimacy issues. The film *Hope Springs (2012)* does both. It features Meryl Streep and Tommy Lee Jones as a mid-life couple stuck in the rut of a boring, passionless routine. Streep's character (Kay) asks that they seek a marriage therapist (played well by Steve Carell). The movie depicts the heartache of rigid marital domestication. The movie characters eventually agree to attend intensive couples therapy and with help their misery and isolation are confronted.

On and off the screen, Meryl Streep embodies the force of wildness. She has mastered a number of difficult and embarrassing moments especially on film. When interviewed by a radio reporter, Meryl was asked how she faked the masturbation scene in *Hope Springs*. In her continued calm transparency, she paused and said to the interviewer "What makes you think I was faking it?"

Men-O-Pause

Meryl always gives me courage. I confess. When writing this sex section, I kept putting it off. It's been a loaded topic at this time in my mid-life. For decades, I've been privately quite content with my sexuality in my corner of the world. Then "the change" came marching in with the *Reality Reaper*. How dare she revamp the entire vista of my physical and sexual outlook!

I know that I'm not alone. When watching the Broadway hit *Menopause: The Musical,* it wasn't just me that was laughing hysterically. The cast of these four midlife women were telling many of our stories through hilarious song and dance moves about hot flashes, chocolate cravings, brain collapse, nocturnal sweating and sexual predicaments. The lyrics parody popular music from the Boomer era, including a notable musical number, "Puff, my God I'm Draggin". With more humor and acceptance, I know the *Reality Reaper* is here to assist in this Men-O-Pause phase. She visits to help me see and to clean up more of my crummy ageist, sexual-stereotypes. Here are a few examples of my own:

» *Things will keep getting worse as I get older.*

» *Forget about a fun sex life after menopause.*

» *Old people who have sex are gross.*

» *It's not realistic to enjoy aging and improve my sex life.*

» *Libido? It's never coming back.*

» *More hormones. Isn't it the answer to everything!?*

Hormonally Charged

My wildness training started back in utero. My mother, like 5 to 10 million other pregnant women were prescribed a synthetic estrogen hormone called **Diethylstilbestrol (DES).** DES is now known to be an endocrine-disrupting chemical, one of a number of substances that interfere with the endocrine system to cause cancer, birth defects, and other developmental abnormalities. The effects of synthetic estrogen poisoning are most severe when exposure occurs during fetal development. **If you're considering hormone therapy to help alleviate the symptoms of menopause, first find out if you've had possible exposure to DES.**

Between 1940 and 1971, medical doctors encouraged pregnant women to take DES "to prevent a miscarriage". However, a study finally conducted in 1953 reportedly showed that DES did NOT reduce the risk of miscarriage, but this extremely high dosage-estrogen drug was still prescribed. In 1958, my own mother was told by her doctor that these pills "would make me or break me". Women were given DES under many different product names and also in various forms, such as pills, creams, and vaginal suppositories. The average regimen for pregnant women was one 125 milligram pill per day, the estrogenic equivalent of 700 of today's birth control pills!

It took until 1971 for DES to be removed from the market after studies showed an increased risk of rare vaginal and cervical cancers in daughters exposed to DES. The drug continued to be prescribed to pregnant women in Europe until 1978. The most deadly aspects of the DES debacle is how long the information took to filter down to the practices of individual medical doctors and how little the general public still knows about it. Additional DES information can be found in Barbara Seaman's book *The Greatest Experiment Ever Performed on Women: Exploding the Estrogen Myth.*

Spicy Factor

In her entertaining book, *Sex and the Seasoned Woman*, Gail Sheehy interviewed "spicy women" who are unwilling to settle for the stereotypical roles of middle age. A spicy, seasoned woman, according to Sheehy, has been marinated in life experience. "She is committed to living fully and passionately in the second half of life. Seasoned women are open to sex, love, dating, dreams, exploring spirituality and revitalizing their marriage as never before."

On a scale of 1 to 10, what is your spicy factor?

What sexual-ageist stereotypes are still rolling around in your head?

Take a moment to write down your thoughts. Don't try to skip this section, like I wanted to do.

The Crone & the Knight

A fable adapted from the work of Jack Kornfield.

Once upon a time there was a Knight of the Round Table who got lost in the woods. He ended up drinking from a sacred well owned by an old, wrinkled *Crone* (an archetypal figure of a wise woman in many cultures). After the Knight drank from her well, the Crone demanded that the Knight marry her. He begged her for another option. Showing him mercy, the Crone replied "You don't have to marry me if you answer this question: "What do women want?"

The Knight made many attempts to answer her question but failed. Being an honorable guy, the Knight agreed to marry the Crone (much to the shock and amusement of the other people in the Kingdom). On the evening of their marriage, she says "Come kiss me". When he does, she turns into a beautiful, younger woman. The Knight is overjoyed. But then she says, "I can only stay like this half the time. So you will need to choose. Would you rather see me as an old hag while we are out in public during the day or have me in our evening bed as this beautiful, younger woman?"

The Knight's anxiety grew as he contemplated his answer for some time. Finally, he turned to the Crone and said "It is your choice. You decide".

The Crone responded with a joyful laugh and said *"This is exactly what women want. We want the freedom to make our own choices! And now we are both liberated from this curse."* And at that moment the spell was lifted completely.

But I'm Too Old

Don't fret. The Wild Woman knows it's not over. It's time to go nose-to-nose with your excuses. When I ask certain clients "Will you let yourself be happier?" They reply "I'm too old". So, I ask another question. "What about your creative dreams?" They repeat "I'm too old to think about that now". I'm convinced the "I'm too old" excuse is the theme song that fuels the anti-aging movement in this country. You can't fool me. **"I'm too old" is usually a smoke-screen to the underlying "I'm too scared."**

Who cares if you're not the bravest, prettiest or sharpest crayon in the box anymore? Your true colors are begging to rip through. Do you really enjoy watching the state of our nation remaining stuck in a bad adolescence? We each have something to teach and we each have something to learn. Remember, there's no one exactly like you on this planet and there never will be ever again. Think about that one.

If you did your pro-aging homework in the previous chapters: facing your age prejudice, recognizing and releasing resentments, removing exhausting people and monitoring your hamster-wheel busyness, then you're ready for this next section. If you're not ready or interested to resurrect your Wild Woman in the following five steps, then take a break. Pull out your journal when you're more rested and ready.

Resurrecting Your Wild Woman

Over twenty years ago, Clarissa Pinkola Estes rocked our world with *Women Who Run with the Wolves*. Her wonderful book, which includes myths and stories of the Wild Woman archetype, is still a mainstay in my traveling library. Dr. Estes helped us to describe our female psyche through story. We each tell a story about ourselves. The following five steps have been developed to help you create a pro-aging story worth sharing.

Step One: Listen to Your Howl

Take some quiet time to listen within. What wild or tame desires are trying to bubble up to the surface? What did you enjoy doing as a child and as an adolescent? What was fun for you? Where did your imagination take you? Let your past serve you by looking back in this way. Write down all that you enjoyed the most.

Presently, what are the things that get you up every morning? What do you really want to feel on a daily basis? What gives you juice? Any special talents or particular areas you are strong in? If you were at the end of your life, what would you need to have accomplished so that you have no regrets about anything? What do you put off doing?

Get clear and write your responses down in your journal. Again, do this without self condemnation. Practice self compassion. Then pick ONE vision that you would like to bring forward in the next four steps.

Step Two: Surround the Dragon

A happy heart and a conscious creative mind are not exempt from producing a negative naysayer voice. Negativity arises because the egoic mind is afraid of change, especially if it's not at the steering wheel. As a protection device, it pumps out limiting beliefs to frighten us from taking action steps toward a dream. You'll know when the negative naysayer has crashed the party. Watch how your mind will tell you things like "You're being ridiculous", "This happiness thing is absurd", "This project is way too expensive to carry out", "You don't have time to do this" and my three personal favorites: "Who do you think you are", "What will people think?" and "It's not good enough".

Surround your dragon. Make a conscious appraisal of your limiting beliefs. When you face what you fear, it reduces the power to control you. Most importantly, re-affirm your true desire about your life and your creative calling.

Now make a list of your top three strengths. What are two additional positive qualities do you possess? Name at least three things you have accomplished in your life. What are you most proud of? Write all of these down in your journal and sit in the company of your glorious supportive self.

Step Three: Cradle your Creative Seedlings

Ideas require a safe nursery where they can incubate and have time to be swaddled. It's best to keep your emerging creative seedlings private for some time. Cradle them well. Treat yourself and vision to positive affirmations, meditation and prayers of gratitude. Like any form of life, your seedlings will grow healthy and strong if you nurture them well.

One of my clients' described it this way "From a plant struggling to grow in a pot that was too small, I have been transplanted to a bigger pot. There's new space now to enjoy the accompanying possibilities." Take as much nursery time as you need, you'll know when it's time to bring your creative ideas out for show and tell.

Then when you're ready, declare the following out loud:

"Okay, it's time. I might not be perfect. My vision or my craft may not be perfect, but I'm good enough. I can enjoy this life and foster my growing creative process. I'm ready!"

Step Four: Be the Oyster with the Pearl

As you take the action steps to bring your vision public, notice the sensations in your body. Are you feeling energized or drained? **Inspiration feels energizing.** If you don't feel uplifted, gently go back to steps One, Two and Three. You may need to unplug from more of your old limited belief system. Don't worry, this is normal.

It was Thomas Edison that said that "Genius is 1 percent inspiration and 99 percent perspiration". *Eat, Pray, Love* author Elizabeth Gilbert described a formula for her own creative process: "99 percent oyster and 1 percent pearl...it's a bargain to get 1 percent inspiration, it's a miracle." Every time you complete an action step toward your creative vision, you are the oyster that is producing a pearl. As you gain more positive visibility, it can make you sweat. It has for me. If you've already survived months and months of hot flashes, perspiration shouldn't be an issue since you know this too shall pass.

Most of all, find your pack. Connect with those who recognize your howl! Strengthen your patience and endurance muscles (I know, it can get wearisome). It's not easy work to surrender the ego, especially when it wants to produce more fear about aging, illness, money or your loved ones. Keep in close contact your creative pro-aging buddy to keep you both on track.

Step Five: Sleep, Leap and Reap!

Self care is essential. A good pro-aging rule of thumb is to "Get more sleep and then leap!" No need for your Wild Woman to be exhausted which is a common excuse to remain invisible. Comedian Robin Williams reminds us playfully, "You're only given a little spark of madness. You mustn't lose it."

As you continue with your life trajectory and if/when your creative leaps are *not* being appreciated by certain others, move along. When needed, apply one of my favorite pro-aging words— **NEXT!** Over fifty years ago, Decca Records turned down the Beatles after an audition declaring, "We don't like their sound and guitar groups are on their way out." Jennifer Hudson, the young singer who was voted off of *American Idol,* ended up stealing the show in the movie, *Dreamgirls.* When asked how she handled her disappointment of being eliminated from *Idol,* Jennifer admitted that it was painful. She cried (a lot) and eventually returned to hope. Jennifer explained "I chose to trust that God had a bigger picture for me than I could see at the time." I guess so. Her performance in *Dreamgirls* landed her an Oscar.

At this point in life, I don't believe in the concept of failure. Perhaps, there has only been a lack of love behind the endeavor. The Universe will remind us when we go down a people-pleasing, passionless, dead-end road that we weren't in love with in the first place. If you find yourself in that situation, turn around. The gift of wildness will always help you find a new open road. Keep your eyes and heart open, the upcoming intersection or roadway may already be named in honor of your Wild Woman.

If you nurture your life, more creative ideas and things will naturally come to you. Enjoy the energy of receiving. If you practice these five steps, the creative muse in your Wild Woman will remain awaken. She will continue to help you sow, grow and enjoy the seeds that that you came here to reap!

Shine or Whine

While in Northern California, Jim and I visited the Henry Cowell Redwoods State Park. I feel such reverence walking among these ancient trees. Some of them are 1400 to 1800 years old. The so-called 'younglings' are several hundred years old. **If you want to be reminded how age can look and feel magnificent, return to Mature Nature.**

Despite unstable hormones, increased body fat and sexual malfunctions, a pro-aging attitude is fed from the power of appreciation. Do you shine or do you whine? If you need more assistance in the shine department, give thanks for something in your life that doesn't need healing.

You're alive! Go to the mirror right now and congratulate your wonderful, aging face. I really mean it. Or start with ONE aspect of your body that you DO LIKE, even if it's an eyeball. Begin to appreciate more what has been provided to you over the years.

I'll use my own example. At the bathroom mirror, I look into my eyes and say out loud: *"Thank you, dear eyes, for allowing me to see all the beauty that I now see. Thank you my dear eyes, for being with me all these years. Thank you for the gift of your sight which allows me to look around and see the faces that I love dearly. Dear eyesight, thank you for giving me visual access to Mother Earth and all her entertaining creatures. Thank you, to my inner eyes for helping me to see this beauty within."*

Maybe you've read this entire chapter and you're still baffled about all this pro-aging talk of inner animal, relational transparency and cradling creativity? I leave with you one final question.

What is your most common escape fantasy? Tell a pro-aging buddy your honest response and I trust that you will be on your Wild way soon.

CHAPTER FIVE

The Gift of Collaboration

"We belong to each other."
—MOTHER TERESA

There once was a Village filled with people who cared greatly for one another. One day, a village woman became very distraught. Her village friends lovingly gathered her up and took her to see the local medicine woman. The medicine woman looked deeply into the troubled woman eyes and asked her these four questions;

- » When did you stop singing?
- » When did you stop dancing?
- » When did you stop sharing?
- » When did you stop visiting the Great Mother?

What I enjoy about this story is the simplicity of the medicine woman's healing questions. Just in the asking, she reminded the village woman of the medicine that kept her healthy. In this story, I also cherish the power of her caring village friends. As the village woman became distressed, they rallied to bring her to the help she needed. The moral of the story: The gift of collaboration can be life-saving.

The Five Gifts of Pro-aging—A Recap

The first gift, **Authenticity,** invites us to look honestly at how we feed into our anti-aging society and approach our own limiting stereotypes. The second gift, **Self-healing** helps to clear the past and allow us to be healthier and more fully present to this day. The gift of **Discernment** is relentless in its reminders to help us keep a clear focus on our own side of the street. The mystery card in our deck of life is the gift of **Wildness.** It is our link to our animal nature and to the creative power that is connected to the entire cosmos. In our crazy, mother-less world, the fifth pro-aging gift arrives: **Conscious Collaborators.** Awakened women are being called to bring the humane back into humanity.

> There are two kinds of people,
> those who do the work and those who take the credit.
> Try to be in the first group;
> there is less competition there.
> —INDIRA GHANDI

Face the Monster: Friend or Foe

Most of you have been tending to your inner life for a very long period of time. Now, it's time to buddy-up on a larger scale! Learning to collaborate with more women naturally brings up the shadow self. Carl Jung described the shadow as "the thing a person has no wish to be". Our shadow self can appear as a friend or foe.

If we try to push it away, it often shows up in our dreams as intruders or attackers from whom we try to flee or who we want to destroy. In Africa, there is a tribe that teaches its children how to face their shadow parts in their dreams. When being chased by a devouring monster, they are instructed to stop running. In their dream, they are encouraged to turn and face the monster, hold out their hand and say, "Give me your gift".

As this African dream method teaches, one doesn't need to avoid or be controlled by the underworld of our minds. We simply need to acknowledge that everyone has a vulnerable underbelly. Denial of our own darker and imperfect aspects leads to projecting one's shadows traits onto others, making them into the 'bad guys'. Hmmm, I think that is called *WAR*. Conscious pro-aging women know the solution is to turn and face one other and listen more. With that awareness in place, one can then hold out a hand and humbly say "Let me learn from you, please give me your gift."

Inner Collaboration

As with the other four gifts of pro-aging, the fifth begins as an inside job. Since I was a little girl, I was always a thirsty camper looking for the meaning of life. When I was seven or so, I was hoping to find it by joining brownie scouts—that lasted less than an hour. These timeless questions rolled around and around in my being: WHO AM I? WHAT AM I DOING HERE? WHAT DO I DO WITH THIS LIFE?

In my early twenties, I was introduced to someone who really helped me answer these fundamental questions. Prem Rawat and his message have profoundly influenced my life for over three decades. In the fifty-plus years that he has been traveling the world, I've been fortunate to visit many places where his growing message of personal peace is warmly received. The following journal entry describes one of these priceless adventures. It's not always been easy to have a living mentor who's not interested in growing my ego and insecurities.

Journal Entry: Australian Outback

September 2012

I am grateful to be sitting in this beautiful and ancient Aussie outback setting, listening to the wind play through the gum trees. I am alive. I am breathing deeply and slowly. I have everything I need. My heart is full. I am in complete peace. Or at least I think I was.

Oh shoot, my mind is starting to ramp up. It's trying to rally me back into my default mode of rushing about, pushing my agenda and creating doubt and fear.

Once again, I lean into my breath. I feel the sensation of my heart giving thanks for being here. There's enough space to honor everything including the hard work and the physical challenges it took for me and many others to get here.

I sit with my fearless teacher, amazing mentor and friend. He's relentless as an ambassador of peace. He's growing by leaps and bounds. Can I say the same about myself? Can I appreciate my own conscious growth? Can I keep feeding this tasteful dish to my heart? Today, Prem Rawat joyfully exhibited the qualities that emanate from a happy soul: humbleness, kindness, gratitude and appreciation.

My mind is not so happy. It is so restless. I am overwhelmed (humbled?) by these changes in my physical self. Today, an Italian older man stood up and spoke. The essence of his request was this, "I'm older now but I am not washed up, please, I'd like to still help with your message of peace". As the older man spoke, I could feel my own inner voice rise up. I TOO DO NOT FEEL WASHED UP!!!

Yet, reality has struck. I look around and see a slew of younger generation sitting in the audience. They are filled with waves of enthusiasm and physical vitality.

I've been ridiculous at this conference. I've been running around trying to prove that I can still "show up and do the job". Yup, I'm a mad woman attempting to go back and reclaim my youth. I'm trying to re-create my experiences from decades ago. Prem will have nothing to do with it.

I watch my mind flopping around like a fish-out-of-water. I've pushed and pushed my physical limitations. For what reason? Because I feel I'm being replaced by a younger generation AND I AM. In part, that is the necessary reality.

So what's an aging student of life to do?

Prem simply smiles as he delivers his reply: "Enjoyment...Receive the gift of Enjoyment... Treasure your timeless heart."

The Patriarchy—Unplugged

Over the last fifty years, American Boomer women have spent more time on therapy couches, meditation cushions and yoga mats than any other group in society. Yet, many still report a huge and frustrating gap between what we feel, what we know and how to really make a difference in our increasingly violent culture. We are more educated, financially successful and accomplished than any generation of women in history. Yet, deep down the majority of us feel like we are still missing the mark. One woman described it this way "I feel about ten months pregnant with no way of getting this baby out!"

There have been reasons for this long pregnancy. For over five thousand years, we've been living under a competitive masculine-based operating system. Globally, we know that this operating system has crashed. It's still trying to re-boot. Struggling to keep the out-dated patriarchy alive, the fear tactics keep rolling in. However, seasoned women know better. We know that fear and competition shut down the kindness of the human heart. Fear and competition also stamps out the art of learning. When a culture is so motivated by a performance-driven model, then the practice of collaborative learning is judged as inferior and something to be avoided.

Pro-aging women are naturally equipped to bring forward a solid, heart-based platform birthed from cooperation, not competition. Lucia Rene, teacher and author of *Unplugging the Patriarchy* serves as an incredible resource. She points out in the last 6,000 years, the essences of our true masculine and feminine roles have become completely reversed. In short, the shadow side of masculine energy has emerged as *entitlement*. The shadow side of feminine energy has surfaced as *self lack*. To help us ALL get back on course, the real essence of the feminine is power and needs to be recognized as such. The most real essence of the masculine comes from the heart, not the mind.

If we continue under the umbrella of an outdated operating system (based on fear, greed and competition) it will be impossible for American woman to truly collaborate. How do you know when you're still buying into the patriarchal rules? When gathering with other woman notice if the following characteristics arise: comparisons, envy, jealousy, paranoia, rigidity and a survival of the fittest mentality. If so, do your inner work! Otherwise, the shadow aspects of the masculine will keep surfacing and shut down the process of conscious collaboration.

Writer-director Woody Allen has brought us genius films about the nature of our human neurosis, especially the competitive "compare and despair game". I'm reminded of a scene from his less popular movie *Stardust Memories*. Woody is sitting on the dingy and dimly lit train surrounded by other anguished and unhappy people. He peers out through the train window. Woody spies another train car across the way, on another parallel train track. Of course, the other is the 'happy train car'. It is brightly lit, filled with beautiful, laughing people sipping their overflowing champagne. At first, he is longingly intrigued with the view. As you can predict, Woody then plummets into despondency as he recognizes the 'happy train car' is out of his league.

Envy sucks. Who hasn't fallen victim to the game of compare and despair? Mark Twain wrote *"comparison is the death of joy"*. The egoic mind loves to weigh and measure everything and everyone. Somewhere between grandiosity and shame, our discernment can flourish when we detach from the pain caused by an insecure ego. **Pro-aging is about helping each other to end this competitive game of compare and despair.**

Three Men on a Hike

Three men were hiking through a forest when they came upon a large raging, violent river. Needing to get to the other side, the first man prayed:

"God, please give me the *strength* to cross this river."'

Poof! God gave him these big arms and strong legs. He was able to swim across the river but it took two hours and he almost drowned twice.

The second man, after witnessing this prayed:

"God, please give me the *strength and the tools* to cross this river."

Poof! God gave him strong arms, strong legs and a rowboat.

He was able to row across the river in about an hour but he almost capsized once.

Seeing what happened to the first two men, the third man prayed:

"God, please give me the *strength, the tools and the intelligence* to cross this river."

Poof! He was turned into a woman.

She checked the map, hiked one hundred yards up stream and walked across the bridge.

Bitches, Whores, Witches & More

History lessons can be infuriating and empowering. Most American Boomer women are clueless about the historical origins of our sex. I know I was. And there is still much to learn. It's not surprising that we've been uninformed since much of women's history was absent or censored from our high school and college history books. The roots of feminine collaboration in our country are fascinating and a bit of a treasure hunt.

To help fill in some of the blanks, I was able to connect with UCLA Women's History professor, Dr. Ellen Dubois. This introduction occurred through the gracious efforts of Marianne Williamson at our first SISTER GIANT conference held in Los Angeles. Dr. Dubois is an expert on American women's history including women's suffrage and feminism. If you read any of her five published books, you will understand more of the truth of who you are as woman and where we came from. It's also thrilling to support Marianne Williamson as she consciously infiltrates our American political arena.

Gather your women friends in the name of conscious collaboration and view these four highly recommended women's media presentations. I'd suggest you show each of these films at a separate weekly gathering. This will allow more time for you to digest and discuss each film. I've listed how you can freely access or purchase a copy of each film in the recommend resources section.

1. ***The Burning Times.*** This documentary is uncomfortable to watch and yet, very important to process as a woman. It covers much of the history of the witch burnings, which occurred around the world. An estimated three to five million (mostly women, but also men and children) were tortured and killed by the "Holy Inquisition", instigated by the Roman Catholic Church. This film speaks volumes as to why many women still fear their voices, reject their healing powers and are reluctant to gather.

My first time watching *The Burning Times* was with 500 other courageous women. It was remarkable and distressing. When the film was over, Marianne guided us through an amazing debrief that allowed a sacred, safe pace for our feelings to surface and to be able to comfort one another in smaller groups. The next morning, I awoke and wrote the following poem.

Women's Voices

The rain outside awoke me with thunderous sounds.
Tears of remembrance spill from these sacred grounds.
Flashes of many thousands of women, children and husbands who died.
All of their grand knowing entombed inside.
Today, we ask for the release from this cycle of pain.
By seeking the Eternal Heart for that we will gain.
Awake once more to a living Miracle.
We gather again in this sacred Circle.
Our voices globally linked as we answer the call.
Here to re-plow this fertile field with peaceful resolve.

2. The second recommended documentary, ***Pray the Devil Back to Hell,*** will have you cheering on the brave women from the country of Liberia. Through their collaborative perseverance, these African women went nose-to-nose with murderous-drug warlords and eventually had them removed from their country. After this remarkable feat, the people of Liberia went on to elect their first woman president. Liberia joined the ranks of fifty-nine women who have become female Presidents of their various countries, dating back since 1940. At the time of this writing, the USA is still not one of them.

3. ***Not For Ourselves Alone*** is a PBS documentary (directed by Ken Burns) of the dramatic, little-known story of the compelling friendship of Elizabeth Cady Stanton and Susan B. Anthony. These two powerful Americans were born into a world ruled entirely by men and fought to improve the lives of women everywhere. This excellent documentary includes compelling interviews and historical photographs never before seen on screen. In America, Elizabeth and Susan will hopefully be remembered as our out-of-the-box forerunners who modeled conscious political collaboration.

> If you think you're too small to be effective, you
> have never been in bed with a mosquito.
> —BETTE REESE

4. ***Iron-Jawed Angels.*** Dr. Ellen Dubois has given her 'thumbs up' to this Hollywood movie due to its accurate portrayal of the women's suffrage movement in the United States. It stars Hillary Swank, Julia Ormand, Anjelica Huston and many other talented actresses. The storyline is about the actual women who fought and went to jail to secure political representation for American women. While grateful for their ground breaking actions, our current American policy-making institutions still lack adequate female representation. We can be inspired by this film knowing that pro-aging women have the full resources to ensure that more of our peers are represented in the political arena.

When you watch each of these films, I'm certain you'll feel a deep connection to these courageous women. Once upon a time there were civilizations where the feminine principle was revered, not feared. For instance, in the pre-Christian civilizations of the Sumerians, Egyptians and Celtics, women were highly respected and their wisdom was sought after. In some Eastern parts of the world, the feminine Hindu Goddess—Lakshmi is recognized *equally* as a source of prosperity, beauty and strength even to God Vishnu.

Female Mentors

Make a list of five influential women whom you most admire.

What attributes and values make you drawn to them?

Are their attributes and values linked to looking young?

Do you currently have a female mentor that is teaching you about healthy collaboration with other women?

A pious soul dies, goes to heaven and gains an audience with the Virgin Mary.

The visitor asks Mary why (with all her blessings) she always seemed to appear in paintings as looking a bit sad, a bit wistful. The new visitor asks the Virgin Mary "Is everything Okay?"

Mary gives her kind visitor a reassuring look and gently replies "Oh, everything's great. No problems. It's just … well……the truth is we had always wanted a daughter."

Kali Yuga

Studies by the United Nations World Bank have shown that women are more likely to contribute to community development than men. Therefore, women are better candidates for support programs. Rock-singer and activist-Bono put it wisely, "Give a man a fish; he'll eat for a day. Give a woman even a micro-credit; she, her husband, her children and her extended family will eat for a lifetime."

Allowing more women to receive increased resources is a key problem around the world. Many ancient cultures have predicted this current time in history: Kali Yuga—*the age of darkness.* 'Kali' to Hindus and Buddhists means "strife, discord, quarrel or contention". Long ago, the Greek civilization described the four ages (stages) of human decline into the Age of Gold, the Age of Silver, the Age of Bronze and the Age of Iron, which we are presently in (no surprise). We know that dignity and respect for human life, especially for women has reached a bottom.

While many of us live comfortable lives which include enough food, access to health care and adequate schools for our children and grandchildren, millions upon millions of people (including in the USA) struggle to meet these simple, basic needs.

*Consider these current facts:

» One out of every six people in the world live on less than one dollar a day; 75 percent of them are women.

» Women produce 50 percent of the world's food, yet own only 1 percent of its land.

» In the U.S., one in four children go to bed hungry or what is termed "food insecure".

» At least 17,000 children die from hunger every day.

» Malnutrition leads to nearly one-third of all childhood deaths before age five.

» 925 million people worldwide do not have enough to eat—that's nearly three times the population of the U.S.

» More than 60 percent of the world's hungry are women

» More than half a million women die from pregnancy-related causes each year.

» One out of every seven Afghan women dies when giving birth because of lack of medical attention.

» Afghan rape victims can be forced by law to marry their attacker.

» African women spend five hours per day (on average) seeking out water and carrying it back to their villages.

» More than 72 million children, mostly girls, lack access to basic, primary education.

» Of the 876 million adults in the developing world who can't read, two-thirds are women.

*Sources: Results.org, CARE.org, TakePart.com, and United Nations Food and Agriculture Organization.

These are staggering statistics, aren't they? When I compiled these facts together, I wept.

Clearly, we have huge problems on our planet, especially for women and children. In the United States, Baby Boomers spend over $3 trillion per year and control 70 percent of the nation's wealth. According to the Boston Consulting Group, **while men still earn more, women control nearly three-quarters of all purchasing decisions.** Judging by other economic indicators, those numbers will only grow for American women.

This is not about making anyone feel guilty for the wealth and privileges we possess. Similar to the medicine woman at the start of this chapter, my role is to simply ask two important pro-aging questions:

1. **How do we want to be remembered as American women?**
2. **Are you ready to help?**

We Have Enough

A recent news story involved a delegation of African male council members, who had just completed their robust technological visit of the Los Angeles area. A journal reporter asked them if they had any comments or questions before leaving.

The African delegates become very quiet and looked at one another. One of the soft-spoken elders stepped forward and replied, "**Why don't the women here speak up to their men and say we have enough? In our village, if the men keep hunting and bring back too much meat, our women declare "No more, we have enough and that will be the end of hunting for awhile."**

The reporters fell silent. There were no more questions.

Source: The original news story provided by Lucia Rene, author of *Unplugging the Patriarchy.*

Fifty Shades of Gray

Born between 1945 and 1964, Boomers have been the forerunners of social, political, and environmental change. The sheer force of the 78 million people in the massive Baby Boomer generation has been described as the *"shockwave"* or *"the pig in the python"*. Boomers have become known as the demographic bulge which has remodeled a society as it passed through it. Through our sheer numbers, purchasing power and experienced wisdom we are capable to bring something forward besides our temperamental bank portfolios.

How about some truly new revolutionary roles for maturity? There's a major problem with this idea. Baby Boomers are in denial about their aging. The concept of pro-aging can be confronting territory for a generation who has decided to be young forever.

In a survey conducted by Pew Research Center, most people said "old age" began at age 68. But those who were over the age of 65 thought it began at 74. **In other words, being old is wherever you haven't gotten to yet.**

The first director of the National Institute of Aging, Dr. Robert Butler, coined the word *ageism* in 1968. He noted, "Ageism allows the younger generations to see older people more different than themselves, thus they subtly cease to identify with their elders as human beings".

Forty-five years later since Dr. Butler's spoke about ageism; we're still trying to deal with the elderly scene. However, there is no "us" and "them". We are now them. Every seven seconds, a Baby Boomer turns 50. By 2023, one in five Americans will be over age 65. That's currently the percentage of seniors in Florida.

How will these "revolutionary roles for maturity" come about? My prediction is that you won't find most Boomers congregating at senior centers, unless we turn them into something else. We're going to do it differently. I don't know how and I don't know where. What I do know is the gift of collaboration can make it happen. Pro-aging pioneer, Maggie Kuhn excelled at conscious collaboration as she and her organization lobbied and litigated against age discrimination. Here's some of her amazing story.

In 1970, when United States law forced Maggie Kuhn to retire at age 65 from her executive position in a Presbyterian Philadelphia Church, colleagues gave her a sewing machine. She never opened the box. Instead, she founded the *Gray Panthers* organization. She and her organization's achievements have been vast, including the repeal of the mandatory retirement law. *Gray Panthers* have continued to lobby and litigate against age discrimination in the areas of retirement, housing and health care.

Before she appeared on a TV talk show, a producer gave Kuhn the idea to name the group after the revolutionary Black Panthers. Her group started out as *The Consultation of Older and Younger Adults for Social Change*. At the time, the group appealed to young adults because of its anti-war stance on the Viet Nam War. In 1970, Kuhn sent a delegate to Hanoi to meet with prisoners of war. Shortly after, the *Gray Panthers* organized care packages to draft resisters who fled to Canada to avoid being arrested for draft evasion.

> *"We are the risk takers, we are the innovators,*
> *we are the developers of new models."*
> —MAGGIE KUHN (1905-1995)
> GRAY PANTHERS FOUNDER

GrayPanthers.org website lists the Founder's intention as *"Age and Youth in Action. We are an intergenerational, multi-issue organization working to create a society the puts the needs of people over profit, responsibility over power and democracy over institutions."* From a one time high of 70,000 members and 85 chapters nationwide (at the time of Kuhn's death), the *Gray Panther* membership has significantly dwindled. Why? You probably don't have to be a sociologist to know the answer.

You're Old, I'm Not

Many Boomers have a hard time calling themselves 'middle-aged', let alone aligning themselves with an organization that has the word 'gray' in it. It reminds me of a recent conversation that I had with a gay male friend (my age). I was sharing with him my enthusiasm about the benefits of being an AARP member. He looked at me in horror at even to the thought of being a card-carrying member.

If you're like many Americans over 50, you think you're *not* like most people over 50. That's the key finding in a recent AARP survey with 1,800 Americans.

Eighty-five percent of respondents told us they're not old yet. One 90-year old woman said a woman isn't "old" until she hits 95. So who is old? It just depends who you ask.

A Different Kind of Crones Disease

The force of aging denial in America and increasingly around the world continues to build. It's rare when the media and the entertainment industry choose to feature positive stories of those in the second half of their lives. Western society is more obsessed with celebrity baby bumps and the newest techniques of how to stop-the-clock. To help aide our pro-aging shift, the work of Rabbi Zalman Schachter-Shalomi is available, even for us gentiles. His book, *Age-ing to Sage-ing* describes a profound vision of growing older. For years, he's been committed to helping reverse the stereotypes that have given old age a bad rap.

Shalomi (or Reb Zalman as he is known by many) describes the difference between *becoming an elder* and *being elderly*. He explains that *elders* go through a process of conscious and deliberate growth. He speaks about *sages* who are capable of guiding their families and communities with heart-earned wisdom. *The elderly*, on the other hand often survive into their eighth and ninth decades plagued by a mounting sense of alienation, loneliness and social uselessness. The *elderly* are those who suffer from their reduced capacities and the erosion of their self-esteem. By Shalomi's standards, the majority of elderly Americans are aging without sage-ing.

Sage-ing International is a part of a broader movement that offers a vision of aging as a time of life characterized not by diminishment and decline, but by growth, contribution and fulfillment. A growing consortium of twelve like-minded organizations, have agreed to support each other in promoting conscious aging thought and action, currently known as the *Conscious Aging Alliance*. They model and support a new vision of aging which includes lifelong learning, healthy lifestyle practices, ecological interests and political activism.

We need to re-build more avenues for older and younger people to socialize, work and volunteer together. Segregation is so old school. It's also ludicrous to expect one spouse, partner, child or caretaker to give what a whole village used to provide. We will always need each other. Clearly, the gift of collaboration is a key ingredient in bringing forth a new vision of empowered aging into the mainstream.

> Never underestimate the power of a small group to change the world.
> In fact, it is the only thing that ever has.
> —MARGARET MEAD

Pro-aging in the Land of Fake

Ladies of America it's time for more positive visibility. Do you really think the 'hotties' being featured in today's media can positively steer our world? I'm not willing to risk it. How about you? As pro-aging women collaborate more, we'll probably be called the "the old girls network", so what. The point being, if we keep waiting for our government or mega-corporations to enhance life on earth, we'll all be dead.

If you practice these five gifts as suggested, it will help turn down the volume of personal and cultural ageism. As you bravely do this internal and external work, you help model a brighter, more mature American culture. This is exactly how new evolutionary roles for maturity will be brought forward; one human being at a time.

More than Just a Girl Thing

Friendship—the feeling of being connected to a supportive network, profoundly affects the health of both genders. Loneliness is one of the principal causes of premature death in this country. According to UCLA social neuroscientists, friendship buffers the hardships of life's transitions; it lowers blood pressure, boosts immunity and even protects us from the effects of dementia.

I'm convinced that women on average have lower rates of heart disease and longer life expectancies than men because we naturally practice and value the art of relationships.

'Team BOOM'

Women's leadership styles are highly effective. We tend to be are more inclusive, empathic and flexible in group settings. To validate this point, a recent research study from the journal of *Science* found that having more women on a team makes the team smarter. What makes a group more intelligent has more to do with the team's interaction. Typically, women encourage participation, share information and power, enhance other people's self worth and are experts at getting others excited about their projects. According to this study, the *social intelligence* of a team has little to do with the brain power of its individual members. In other words, it's no surprise that women score high on social sensitivity.

Based on my work with effective groups over the years, I recommend the following guidelines to foster collaborative learning, leadership and teamwork. These are feminine (heart-based) principles to the core. I guarantee that if you come together and follow these guidelines, you'll have loads of more fun playing on this type of team.

Guidelines to Foster Collaborative and Effective Teamwork:

» Check your ego when arriving at the front door.

» Commit to extending and receiving a high level of dignity, respect and non-competition.

» Listen to one another—*really listen.*

» Learn to get along with others by doing your emotional processing (inner work) outside of team meetings.

» Move beyond solo project thinking into we-culture thinking.

» Plunge into the deep pool of inspired creativity that flows from the collective.

» Emerge with simple ideas, identify adequate tools and write down the sustainable steps necessary to make this conscious change happen.

» Feel the aliveness that is released when everyone is empowered with participation.

» Enjoy and celebrate the team outcomes.

Be of good service and you will always have a job.

A few years back, Prem Rawat shared an Egyptian mythical story that has stayed with me. According to the myth, before passing into the afterlife you are asked two questions;

Firstly, did you find real joy in this life?

Secondly, did you help others to find that real joy?

If are able to answer 'yes' to both questions, then you were able to pass into heaven.

Pro-ager's aren't willing to wait until the pearly gates to experience "heaven". Why not co-create a little bit more of heaven on earth today?

Pro-Aging Vision Exercise

Instructions: Block off one hour of uninterrupted time just for you. Read over the instructions and reflect on the questions listed below. After doing so, close your eyes. Try to follow the coming and going of your breath. Don't worry if your monkey-mind starts jumping all over the place. A friend of mine calls it her "wild horses" and she allows them to run until her mind settles down. Employ the best centering technique that works for you.

If you're doing this Pro-aging Vision exercise by yourself (and not in a facilitated group), first read each of the questions slowly. Then take a moment and ask your Highest Self to respond. Notice what information comes forward easily and what feels like resistance. If your thoughts resemble those of Chicken Little's ("the sky is falling"), that's not your Highest Self. Sit some more within the simplicity of your breathing. Read the question again. Take as long you need to hear, see and feel your response from a calm place within your being. As you read each question, write out any images, thoughts, feelings or sensations as they arise.

When you're ready, take out your journal. Remember to include today's date at the top of the page. It can be fascinating to go back and review the evolution of your pro-aging journey. You can repeat this *Pro-Aging Visions Exercise* periodically, to help you manifest and more fully embody your responses. Another option is to create a Pro-Aging Visions Board. This involves creating a visual colorful representation (or collage) on poster board of your responses to this exercise.

Most of all, take your time in completing this Vision exercise. Allow the sweetness of your personal truths to flow freely through you.

> » What does being authentic mean to me?
>
> » How can I bring more of my authentic self into my vision of aging?
>
> » When I think about living longer, what feelings would I like to embrace?
>
> » What am I doing to promote my health?
>
> » How do I want to be able to move in my body as I grow older?
>
> » What am I avoiding in my body that needs attention?
>
> » As I see myself growing older do I envision more self acceptance?
>
> » What is important to me?
>
> » What meaningful work and fun activities am I involved in?
>
> » What fulfilling activities do I see myself involved with as I grow older?
>
> » How is my financial health today?

» How much money is enough for the future? What does "enough" look like to me?

» Do I feel loved? By whom?

» Who do I most enjoy being with? Who do I love?

» Do I feel love for myself?

» How do I express my love and care?

» How do others fit into my pro-aging vision?

» What are my regrets? What have I learned from them?

» Do I feel hurt by others and require more healing assistance?

» Who have I hurt?

» Who do I still need to make peace with?

» Have I accomplished what I came here to do? What is that?

» How content do I feel today?

» Higher Self, what key message do you want me to understand today?

After completing this exercise, take a quiet break. Afterwards, it's important that you share your Pro-Aging Vision responses and vision board with a trusted other. It's important to speak and share your vision out loud. This affirms your precious human life and grounds your connection to the greater good. If possible, set up a weekly check-in with a pro-aging buddy, or create an ongoing buddy group to support your life enjoyment each day and your unfolding vision.

> *"Vision without action is a daydream.*
> *Action without vision is a nightmare."*
> —JAPANESE PROVERB

Choose What Has Chosen You

Ubuntu is an African philosophy that states "I am what I am because of who we all are". Ubuntu is characterized by an awareness of our interconnectedness as human beings. We all have an innate need for peace, compassion and integrity. When it comes to the social herd, pro-aging women have the ability to inspire and insist upon actions of integrity. To repeat, we must each face our own shadows of grandiosity, greed and entitlement. They need to be called out and cleaned up. Likewise, we must each face our feminine shadow that instructs us that we lack something and we must sacrifice our powers of knowing. We can find freedom from the addiction to unnecessary suffering. In doing so, we can evolve as a pro-aging species and brighten the social mood with Ubuntu.

Our natural state is based in simplicity. With each passing day, I increasingly come to realize how extraordinary human existence is. When I accept my aging life on life's terms, more of my suffering is replaced with serenity. Are you interested in embracing the awesome being that you already are? Then simply choose what has already chosen you.

Synonyms of **Awesome** (adjective)

Synonyms: breathtaking, splendid, tremendous, remarkable, amazing, awe-inspiring, fearsome, astounding, humbling.

bing.com—Bing Dictionary

The Pro-Aging Women's Credo™

We recognize what life is offering us today. We are a vital generation of women committed to living fully in the second half of our lives. We don't buy into the old aging stereotypes nor endorse today's youth worshiping. We have stepped into more loving acceptance of our bodies. No longer distracted by the needs of ego, we are free to comfortably age and enjoy our lives.

We are responsible for our own wellness. We ask, receive and give healing support. We face our emotional triggers and in so doing, they dissolve. No longer manipulated by guilt and fear, we rise to the truth of our own value and visibility. We strive to make peace with all of our past. As midlife women we have paid our dues. We relish in this glorious moment. We relax, breathe and laugh more loudly.

Today, we are the lightworkers, the peace bearers. We are the mid-wives for this New Pro-Age. In these transitional times, we are the women who bring clarity to the chaos. We are both still and skilled. Where we visit, more harmony follows. We are savvy and knowing.

Our clarity accompanies us into all the places we visit including boardrooms, bedrooms and beyond. We embody teamwork. We appreciate and nurture our chosen tribe of friends, family and those within our collaborative circles. We help each other out. We've always heard the cries of Mother Earth and are active participants in healing our planet. We pick a spot on the planet and feed it. We don't tell you what to do; we show you.

A Personal Affirmation version of the Pro-Aging Woman's Credo™ is available in the Appendix.

Waiting for Permission?

It's time to pull out your journal one last time. Thank you for bringing forth your honesty and courage when responding to these timely questions.

1. What does integrity mean to you? Where do you find it most in your life?

2. How can the gifts of authenticity, self-healing, discernment and/or wildness help to produce an effective change for you? If so, what is your next step with one or more of these gifts?

3. What does conscious collaboration mean to you?

4. Do you feel this pro-aging book and exercises may be helpful to explore and discuss with others?

5. Do you want to take part in making changes in our current culture of anti-aging? If so, how?

6. What other pro-aging ideas do you have that may be helpful and timely?

7. How can I and others help you with your own *Pro-Aging Vision*?

8. Are you still waiting for someone's permission to proceed?

Free to Stay and Free to Go

Journal Entry:

In the freshness of the still morning, I awoke and walked across our bedroom floor. A new message traveled into my awareness, *"I've already done what I've come here to do."*

I stopped in the middle of the room. Inhaling, I allowed these words to settle into my being. As I exhaled, I felt a new surprising level of relief and relaxation.

Curious to explore this message some more, I grabbed my journal. The pen seemed to automatically write out these words: *"I'll say it to you again; you've already done what you've come here to do. You're free to stay and you're free to go."*

I paused and asked, what is it that I came here to do? What is it that I've already done? And what's this kinda freaky "free to go" statement?

The pen writes on auto-reply. *"What you came here to do was to discover the deepest love possible. You're linked to the most beautiful love within. This love is growing like a breathtaking perennial garden that's been tended to for years. Recognize and honor this ongoing beautiful gift."*

Waves of bliss rolled over me as I realized the truth of this message. I then heard myself exclaim *"I'm free! I feel liberated! I can stay or I can go!"* I then jumped around the room until I ran into our dresser drawer.

While rubbing the reality of my bumped thigh, I asked "OK, then what's keeping me from fully joining back into the light?"

Once again the pen response flowed quickly and easily. *"Oh, that's pretty simple. It's the joy factor. It's about falling deeper in love here on Earth. There's more sweetness to be felt and you can help spread it around. But Dear One, keep it simple—please."*

Source Heals. Love Rules. Do Your Part.

Thank you so much for choosing to read and reflect on the five gifts of pro-aging as offered. Perhaps, you're already planning a *Pro-aging Circle* to openly discuss this material with others. I invite you to share your own *Ageist to Awesome* stories and glories. No doubt, there will be many more gifts to be revealed. It's been said if you hear something once that touches you, listen to it. If you hear it a second time, enjoy it. If you hear it a third time, use it. For each pro-aging action you take, another woman in America and another person around the world will benefit. It's called the ripple effect. Remember, the real strength of mankind has always begun with women. My love travels to you always.

> **One final message about Pro-Aging:**
>
> Well, crap...
> I forgot what it was.
>
> Oh yeah, keep your sense of humor about all of it.

Recommended Resources

Going Gray: How to Embrace Your Authentic Self with Grace and Style by Anne Kreamer, Little Brown and Company, 2007.

The Age of Miracles: Embracing the New Midlife by Marianne Williamson, Hay House, 2008.

Fierce With Age: Chasing God and Squirrels in Brooklyn by Carol Osborn, Turner Publishing, 2013.

The Secret Pleasures of Menopause by Christine Northrup, M.D., Hay House, 2008.

Relax—Your May Only Have A Few Minutes Left: Using the Power of Humor to Overcome Stress in Your Life and Work, by Loretta LaRoche, Hay House, 2008.

Saying Yes To Change: Essential Wisdom for Your Journey by Joan Z. Borysenko, Ph.D., and Gordon F. Dveirin, Ed.D., Hay House, 2006.

From Age-Ing to Sage-Ing: A Profound New Vision of Growing Older by Zalman Schachter-Shalomi, Warner Books, 1995.

Women Who Run With the Wolves: Myths and Stories of the Wild Woman Archetype by Clarissa Pinkola Estes, Ph.D., Ballantine Books, 1992.

Anam Cara: A Book of Celtic Wisdom by John O'Donohue, HarperCollins Publishers, 1997.

Inventing The Rest of Our Lives: Women in Second Adulthood by Suzanne Braun Levine (former Editor of Ms Magazine), Plume Publishing, 2005.

Sex and the Seasoned Woman: Pursuing the Passionate Life by Gail Sheehy, Random House, 2006.

No Ordinary Box—An edited compilation of 20 talks of Prem Rawat delivered to live audiences, without script or rehearsal. Adi Book, 2013, Words of Peace Global—*www.wopg.org.*

Why People Don't Heal and How They Can by Caroline Myss, Harmony Books, 1997.

The Baby Boomer Diet by Donna Gates, Hay House, 2011.

The Reconnection: Heal Others, Heal Yourself by Dr. Eric Pearl, Hay House, 2001.

The Greatest Experiment Ever Performed On Women: Exploding the Estrogen Myth by Barbara Seaman, Hyperion, 2004.

Counter Clockwise: My Year of Hypnosis, Hormones, Dark Chocolate, and Other Adventures in the World of Anti-Aging by Lauren Kessler, Rodale Press, 2013.

Through Women's Eyes, Combined Volume: An American History with Documents (3rd Edition) by Ellen Carol Dubois and Lynn Dumenil, Bedford St. Martin's Press, 2012.

Recommended Women's Documentaries/Movie Information

The Burning Times.
National Film Board of Canada, 1990
Running Time: 56 minutes.
Free viewing, DVD purchase and Download:
http://www.nfb.ca/film/burning_times/

Pray the Devil Back to Hell
A Film by Abigail Disney and Gini Reticker, 2008
Running Time: 53 minutes
Free viewing: *http://www.pbs.org/wnet/women-war-and-peace/full-episodes/*
pray-the-devil-back-to-hell/
DVD purchase: www.praythedevilbacktohell.com

Not For Ourselves Alone
Florentine Films & PBS Series, 1999
Running Time: 108 minutes
Free Viewing or purchase: *http://www.pbs.org/stantonanthony/*

Iron-Jawed Angels
HBO Film, 1994
Directed by Katja von Garnier
Running Time: 125 minutes

Appendix

Personal Affirmation
The Pro-Aging Woman's Credo™

I recognize what life is fully offering me today. I am part of a vital generation of women committed to living fully in the second half of my life. I do not buy into the old aging stereotypes nor endorse today's youth worshiping. I have stepped into more loving acceptance of my body. No longer distracted by the needs of ego, I am free to comfortably age and enjoy my life.

I am responsible for my own wellness. I ask, receive and give healing support. I face my emotional triggers and in so doing, they dissolve. No longer manipulated by guilt and fear, I rise to the truth of my own value and visibility. I strive to make peace with all of my past. As a midlife woman I have paid my dues. I relish in this glorious moment. I relax, breathe and laugh more loudly.

Today, I am part of the lightworkers, the peace bearers. I am a mid-wife for this New Pro-Age. In these transitional times, as a woman I bring clarity to the chaos. I am both still and skilled. Where I visit, more harmony follows. I am savvy and knowing.

My clarity accompanies me to all the places I visit including boardrooms, bedrooms and beyond. I embody teamwork. I appreciate and nurture my chosen tribe of friends, family and those within my collaborative circles. I am part of a team that helps each other out. I've always heard the cries of Mother Earth and I'm an active participant in healing our planet. I pick a spot on the planet and feed it. I don't tell you what to do; I show you.

An Invitation to Stay Connected

Visit *www.MarciaNewman.com* to sign up for her free *Gifts of Pro-Aging* E-newsletter

Join the conversation at *Gifts of Pro-Aging* on Facebook at:
www.facebook.com/groups/giftsofproaging.
You can click on the button that says "Join Group".

For information on upcoming *Gifts of Pro-Aging* classes, professional talks, seminars, retreats and individual consultations visit: *www.MarciaNewman.com*

If you would like to contact Marcia Newman directly, her email address is:
Marcia@MarciaNewman.com